LEFT ALIVE

LEFT ALIVE

After a Suicide Death in the Family

By

LINDA ROSENFELD

Coordinator and Counsellor
Suicide Attempt Counselling Service
Greater Vancouver Mental Health Service
Vancouver, British Columbia, Canada

and

MARILYNNE PRUPAS

Journalist and Former Counsellor
Suicide Attempt Counselling Service
Greater Vancouver Mental Health Service
Vancouver, British Columbia, Canada

With a Foreword by

Paul E. Termansen, M.D.

Clinical Associate Professor of Psychiatry
University of British Columbia
Member, National Task Force on Suicide
Vancouver, British Columbia, Canada

CHARLES C THOMAS • PUBLISHER
Springfield • Illinois • U.S.A.

Published and Distributed Throughout the World by
CHARLES C THOMAS • PUBLISHER
2600 South First Street
Springfield, Illinois 62717

© *1984 by* CHARLES C THOMAS • PUBLISHER
ISBN 0-398-04953-X
Library of Congress Catalog Card Number: 83-24220

With THOMAS BOOKS *careful attention is given to all details of
manufacturing and design. It is the Publisher's desire to present books that
are satisfactory as to their physical qualities and artistic possibilities and
appropriate for their particular use.* THOMAS BOOKS *will be true to
those laws of quality that assure a good name and good will.*

Printed in the United States of America
SC-R-3

Library of Congress Cataloging in Publication Data

Rosenfeld, Linda.
   Left alive.

   Bibliography: p.
   1. Suicide.   I. Prupas, Marilynne.   II. Title.
RC569.R67   1984   362.8'2   83-24220
ISBN 0-398-04953-X

For my father, Joseph Simon, whose concern for people and desire to write about that concern was his legacy to me.

L.R.

To the memory of my beloved father, Charles Bloome, whose understanding and encouragement I will always cherish.

M.P.

FOREWORD

Left Alive: After a Suicide Death in the Family is an extraordinary book, and I am very pleased to have the honour of presenting this book by Linda Rosenfeld and Marilynne Prupas. The book grew out of pain—pain of the survivors of the suicide of a "significant other," and pain of those who have attempted suicide, as well as the pain of those who try to help others deal with the emotional torment that precedes and follows suicide.

In my own work as a practising psychiatrist, I have long been familiar with the many faces of suicide. A great deal of my own work was initially directed towards the prevention of suicide. I was deeply involved in establishing a local crisis and suicide prevention center. It was already clear then that such a center engaged in the prevention of suicide to a very small extent only. I was, nonetheless, hopeful that such a center would have some impact on the suicide rate. My next project became the establishing of S.A.F.E.R., an acronym for Suicide Attempt Follow-up Education Research. The hypothesis was very simply that those who attempted suicide were at a greater risk of dying by suicide and that direct and immediate counselling would minimize that risk. Experience with S.A.F.E.R. since its inception has borne out that assumption. My experience of working closely and over long periods of time with people who are in a high risk category has led me to accept that suicide amongst this group of people is an inevitable accompaniment of such work. Both Linda and Marilynne have been associated with S.A.F.E.R. for a long time. This book was a natural outgrowth of their work, counselling those who had attempted suicide. The two authors and I held the very first local "survivors" workshop. The idea of working with those who had been left to live is very old and, undoubtedly, has its roots in the intuition of helpers past. I had talked about working with survivors for several years but, for a variety of reasons, somehow never got around to doing it. Most importantly, though, I refrained because of the fact that I had not accepted suicide and feared facing an audience of survivors. When one focuses on the prevention of suicide, it is difficult to face the fact that one is not always successful and must face the consequences of failing. *Left Alive* has grown out of the acceptance of the importance and value of counselling for those at risk for suicide and out of an acceptance that suicides have occurred and will continue to occur and significantly alter the lives of those who have been left to live.

The authors of this book took that initial workshop for the survivors of suicide and developed and nurtured further workshops and groups, reaching wider and wider audiences. The importance of such initiative cannot be underestimated in this field, for those who attempt suicide and those who bear the unresolved emotional conflicts of suicides past are poorly equipped emotionally to seek help and to lay bare their anguish and sorrow. Survivors need to be made aware that help is there and that they are not alone. Clinical workers in the mental health field tend to shy away from working with the suicidal. The work is indeed stressful, filled with uncertainty, tension, and the ever present unpredictability of suicide that defies all expertise.

It takes not only courage to carry on year after year counselling the suicidal but also a strongly supportive peer group and a personal philosophy about life and death that can withstand the constant onslaught of people in pain and on the verge of terminating their existence. The authors of this book possess all of that.

Left Alive will fill a gap in the lives of all those who are involved with suicide. In the end, we all are.

PAUL E. TERMANSEN, M.D.

INTRODUCTION

Our aim in writing this book is to help lessen the pain for the survivor of suicide—the person who is left behind when a loved one kills himself or herself. We do not wish to deal with the *meaning* of suicide or the question of the *right* to suicide but rather to look at what happens to those who are bereaved and what helps them.

For many years we have been working with people who have made a suicide attempt. We have talked with thousands of people who have thought, however briefly, of suicide as a "way out."

In 1971, a suicide attempt counselling service recognized the person attempting suicide as requiring a special kind of counselling. The program grew and expanded during the years to meet new needs as they were recognized. We were counsellors at the inception of this program and began to observe that many of the people attempting to kill themselves were survivors of a suicide death in their family. What we noticed was that these people carried around a burden made up of combined unresolved grief, anger, and self-blame and that they had not been able to shed this burden. We know unresolved grief festers like an open wound, and in times of future loss the pain returns, leaving one unable to cope in a healthy manner. So, the survivor was recognized as having special needs that we want to address.

In 1979 there were 27,640 recorded suicide deaths in the United States and 3,475 recorded in Canada. There are probably ten times that number in reality. Thousands are never reported as suicide, listed instead as accidental, and many single car motor vehicle accidents are considered by suicidologists as unreported suicides. From these statistics we can estimate the huge number of people affected by suicide deaths.

In any time of bereavement there are a multitude of feelings that are engulfing, which then recede to be replaced with others. But it appears that after a suicide death, guilt and anger linger longer and are more oppressive than with other forms of bereavement. What, besides understanding, would lighten this burden? As counsellors we know that sharing feelings that one has not been able to share previously enables people to start the mourning process and to do the necessary grieving to go on with their own lives. This is especially true when sharing with others who have had similar experiences. Because our society generally has difficulty with any grieving process and particularly with the grieving of a suicide death, the self-help or mutual-help groups have evolved. These groups validate human feelings and make them understandable. For those who do not have this opportunity to join a group and do not know where to go to find solace through sharing, for the hundreds of thousands of significant others to suicide deaths, and for those helpers—doctors, friends, social workers, etc.—who come in contact with these people bereaving a suicide death; we hope to give you the opportunity to share the experiences of others through this book. Becoming aware of what has helped others may in turn be helpful to you.

The first chapter of the book is the scenario of a characteristic suicide death that sets the stage for the journey that the bereaved travels from the initial shock to acceptance. The stages in between are covered in the following chapters as we take a look at the unique problems in losing a spouse, a child, a parent, and a brother or sister. The final chapter looks at the recovery stage and a specific helping process.

From our conversations with survivors, we use actual case studies and include creative works in the form of stories and poetry from those who have been left alive.

Because over twice as many men kill themselves as women do, and because the majority of the survivors we have talked with have been women who have lost husbands or sons, we have decided to refer to the suicide victim as *he* throughout the book.

PROLOGUE

The history of suicide in Christian Europe is the history of official outrage and unofficial despair.

—A. Alvarez,
The Savage God

Throughout the history of mankind suicide has been treated as a unique phenomenon with moral, economic, and religious implications. Although much has been written about self-destruction, almost nothing has been mentioned about how the suicidal act itself has affected the bereaved emotionally throughout time and very little about its effect on them culturally and economically.

Life and death were difficult concepts for primitive man. He had to move from the belief that death was due to the influence of spiteful or savage supernatural forces to the idea that man could kill animals or other men. This would have been a long developmental process. Then man had to learn that the ways of killing another would not necessarily be suitable ways for killing oneself. The next development that was to make suicide possible was man's awareness of himself as an individual—a separate entity and not an integral part of the clan. (Choron, 1972).

We can assume that once these developments took place primitive man had the means to incorporate suicide into his culture. From what is known it appears that primitive man used suicide as a method of revenge. He believed his ghost would destroy his enemy, or his act would force his relatives to destroy his enemy for him, or the ritual of the tribe would demand his enemy kill himself in the same way. The act was performed with a ritual consequence in mind. We can only imagine the result to the survivors that this implicit demand made upon them.

Because some primitive tribes believed evil energy was concentrated in the dead body, the corpse was often degraded in some manner. (Alvarez, 1971). There is no available documentation of how the tribe dealt with the bereaved.

The first known document dealing with suicide is an ancient Egyptian text known as *Dispute over Suicide*. In this work, social isolation and loneliness emerge as the main reason for contemplating suicide. Death was also attractive at that time because it was believed to lead to another state of existence in which justice would prevail (Pritchard, 1950).

There have always been questions of immortality and its relation to suicide. The Old Testament contains no promise of immortality, and there are only six recorded suicides in that document. This, however, could have more to do with the positive attitudes to life of the ancient Hebrews and their belief in God's wisdom and justice. At this time in man's search for meaning he came to believe that those who destroyed themselves were temporarily deranged.

This attitude gradually changed, as it does again and again throughout the ages, so that by the time of Homer, the ancient Greeks considered suicide a fitting and reasonable solution to difficult life situations. They considered the most reasonable excuses for self-destruction were dishonor and unrequited love, or death of a loved one.

After the Homeric period, somewhere around the fifth century BC, the outlook on life changed and life was considered not worth living at all. Death was desirable because it fullfilled the soul's wish to rejoin the divine source. This view possibly and probably derived from the savage cruelty of men towards one another.

It appears that between the seventh and fourth centuries BC cynicism and disillusionment with life were widespread (Choron, 1972).

The classical Greek who wished to kill himself would state his reasons to the Senate and request official permission. This would be granted if one's life was hateful or overwhelmed with grief; that is, if external circumstances were intolerable (Alvarez, 1971).

The question of what were acceptable reasons for suicide underwent a change in the later Roman Empire, and the question became, "How to kill oneself with the greatest dignity?" The way one died was more important than death itself. During the rule of Caesar Augustus (around 42 BS to 37 AD) there supposedly existed a sect that preached suicide. However, suicide was acceptable only if there was a cause that was acceptable to the culture. An interesting occurrence as result of this attitude was that between 55 and 117 AD if a criminal was executed for his crimes his property was confiscated. If he killed himself before execution by the state, he was able to safeguard his fortune and pass it on to his relatives (Choron, 1972). He also received a proper funeral. This is one instance where we have some knowledge of the misfortunes of the survivors, and ironically, they benefit, at least economically.

The early Christians were promised sublime immortality in the New Testament in which there is also no prohibition of suicide. Life itself was important and constantly a temptation to sin. At the same time, death was anticipated as a release from life and regarded as entry to a blissful afterlife. Temptation to suicide must have been very high.

Approximately at the time of the fourth and fifth centuries martyrdom was a ticket to paradise. Sacrifice was considered very different than suicide. A martyr knows he will die but dies for a value held by the group. This value is more important than the individual himself, so he becomes a hero—his death arouses admiration and praise (Cain, 1972). The soldier who dies in order to take his enemy with him and the ship's captain who goes down with the ship—these individuals become legends.

So if life itself was full of sin, and suicide was allowable to avoid sin, if martyrs were respected and afterlife was anxiously awaited, suicide became the only logical course. The church had to begin to reject suicide, and it necessarily became a mortal sin. In the sixth century the church legislated against it. The biblical authority was the Sixth Commandment, "Thou shalt not kill," and the act was considered self-murder. The logic went like this: If he killed himself to atone for his sins, he was usurping the function of the state and church. If he died innocent to avoid sin, then he had his innocent blood on his hands, a worse sin than any he might commit, as it was impossible for him to repent.

In the Renaissance period, the fourteenth and fifteenth centuries, again we find a drastic change in attitude. The men and women of this period were very sensitive to the beauty of the world, and the feeling that life was wonderful pervaded their thoughts and actions. People became aware that they were masters of their own destiny. But as man became more aware of life's inevitable transition towards death. This evoked fear and depression.

By the seventeenth century, suicide, by law, was made profitable for the state. We now begin to get an idea of the repercussions suffered by the kin of a suicide. In France, the official legal code stated that the suicide's castle was to be demolished and his name defamed. In England a suicide was declared a *felon*. In both countries his property reverted to the crown. In France, the confiscation of the suicide's property and defamation of his memory finally disappeared with the revolution. In England, the laws confirming confiscation of property were not changed until 1870, and a suicide attempter was still liable to punishment by imprisonment as late as 1961. In Canada, that law, although almost never enforced, was still in effect until 1972. *Suicide* was an illegal act as late as 1954. When suicide was no longer considered a crime, suicide attempts were still considered criminal acts until 1972, even though the punishments were almost never enforced. At present, "aiding and abetting a suicide" is still illegal and is all that remains of suicide and the criminal code (Bolt, 1976). Suicide as an "insane act" was evolved by lawyers as protection against the absurdity of the law since a verdict of felon would deny the dead man of the rites of religious burial and deprive his inheritors of his estate.

The irony of all this is that if the person in emotional pain and turmoil who feels that nothing could be worse than it already is, attempts to kill himself and fails, he would then be considered a criminal; and if he succeeds, he leaves his family a legacy of supposed insanity.

In the nineteenth century, the issue of rightness or wrongness of suicide began to yield to the question of its causes. The philosophers have argued that the true reason for suicide is the refusal to submit to suffering. For the Christian, suffering is justified as a means of salvation and a promise of immortality (Choron, 1972). But whether one should or should not suffer and why some are better able to suffer than others are not questions that can easily be answered, if at all.

In North American culture *problems* are the cause of suicide, and the survivor is forced into searching into his relationship with the deceased to determine if he was part of the problems (Cain, 1972). If we remember that primitive man had some magical belief in revenge happening through the suicidal act itself, then perhaps the survivor of today who feels "it was done to punish me" is in touch with the same manipulative myth. However, while the primitive response to suicide was based on a fear of the vengeful dead, this century's response is probably more related to fear of death itself.

It appears that in twentieth century North America, a verdict of death by suicide, because of a kind but misguided wish to protect the bereaved from this shame and stigma, is often not reported as such. It may be defined as an accident, and we can then say "it was God's will" or "I had no control over it." Suddenness and unpreparedness are part of both accident deaths and suicide deaths, but accidents are easier to accept. The hardest thing of all for the bereaved is not to know if it was or was not a suicide death. Once he knows for certain, he can then focus his feelings around it. Since in 80 to 85 percent of all suicides there is no note, the first question is: "Did he, in fact, kill himself?" One of the most recent ways our society has devised to deal with this question is the "psychological autopsy." This is a series of interviews with the families, friends, and acquaintances of the deceased to try to get a picture of his medical history, recent state of mind, previous suicide attempts, relationships, and total life situation shortly before his death. These interviews are conducted by a special team and are called in by the medical coroner when a death is classified as of *undetermined cause*. This has been especially useful in differentiating accidental drug overdoses and can in many cases lessen the trauma for the bereaved (Choron, 1972). However, this is a relatively new practice and done in only a few places in North America. It does, however, reflect our need to study suicide.

The shift from individual to society, from morals to problems, came with the behavioral sciences of psychology and sociology. Suicide has evolved into an abstract problem for the philosopher or a medical problem for the psychiatrist and is still mostly rejected by society as a human problem. What seems to offend society most about suicide is that the self-destroyer has consulted no one about his decision but has used individual initiative to make a choice alone and in doing so, rejects society and its group values (Halbwachs, 1978). Because we suspect it, not respect it, our cultural way of dealing with suicide has made the survivor the real victim.

"What was once a mortal sin has become a private vice, something shameful to be avoided and unmentionable, less self-slaughter than self-abuse" (Alvarez, 1971).

BIBLIOGRAPHY

Alvarez, A.: *A Savage God: A Study of Suicide*. Des Plaines, Illinois, Bantam Books, 1971.

Boldt, Menno: A Model for Suicide Prevention: The Alberta Task Force Proposals. *Alberta Psychology* 11(4) 1982.

Cain, Albert: *Survivors of Suicide*. Springfield, Thomas, 1972.

Choron, Jacques: *Suicide*. New York, Charles Scribner's, 1972.

Halbwachs, Maurice: *The Causes of Suicide*. English translation published 1978 by Routledge and Kegan Paul Ltd., London, England. First French Publication, 1930.

Pritchard, James, ed.: *Ancient New Eastern Texts*. Princeton, New Jersey, Princeton University Press, 1950.

ACKNOWLEDGMENTS

There are many people we wish to thank for making this endeavor possible.

We are grateful to Paul Termansen, whose dedication to people and faith in our ability to help gave us the confidence to begin.

Our friends and coworkers at S.A.F.E.R., whose continued support and valuable input provided a constant source of stimulation and became essential to the completion of the manuscript.

We acknowledge the greatest debt to all the survivors who shared with us their pain and their creativity, and who became the driving force behind this book.

We especially want to thank

Sheila Diakiew for her contributions on pages 57–63.

Marion Burbank for her "Reflections" on pages 35–36.

Garth Burbank for his introduction to Chapter IX.

Ruth, Brad, and Lillian for their frequent help.

Very special thanks to Paul Belserene, whose unique ability to act as an editor while reacting as a survivor enabled us to put together this material. We also appreciate his written contributions on pages 27, 75–77, 81–83, and 94–96.

We also wish to thank Dawnbreaker Music Company for allowing inclusion of lyrics to "Where Do I Go From Here," by Parker McGee, © 1977 Dawnbreaker Music Company.

Appreciation also goes to Isabella Briski, who contributed endless time typing, made suggestions, and continually injected us with her enthusiasm.

We also want to thank our husbands, Michael and David, and our children, who continued to encourage us even when the time commitments became enormous.

The opportunity to encounter survivors and acquire the knowledge and skills to write about their problems came from the administrative agency that employs us — The Greater Vancouver Mental Health Service.

CONTENTS

LEFT ALIVE

I never saw any point in trying to hide it; things that are dealt with openly are so much more quickly healed than things that are burrowed under.

—Widow survivor

Chapter I

RICHARD KILLED HIMSELF TODAY

A 34 year old man died today of a possible self-inflicted gunshot wound in his home in suburban Toronto. A police spokesman confirmed that Richard Storey apparently committed suicide while his wife and children were out of the house. Neighbours called police to investigate after they heard a loud explosion. Storey is survived by his wife, Elizabeth, and 2 children.

At 11:25 AM Richard put the gun in his mouth and pulled the trigger. The shot not only went upward through his brain but outward to encircle many lives, and the sound will reverberate for many generations. Like all people who die before their time, Richard will be caught in history forever as a young man, but for those who cared about him that picture will be clouded with images of blood and sensations of pain—Richard's blood, his survivors' pain.

Richard had taken the day off from the department store where he was a salesman. Early that morning he had told his wife, Elizabeth, that he did not feel up to facing people. Elizabeth went grocery shopping at 10:20 and in that hour of being alone, surrounded by his possessions and memories, Richard made an ultimate decision about his life and about the value of life itself. He may have made the decision earlier, but it will never be known the exact moment when he entered the cellar of suicide from which he could not find his way out. Elizabeth returned at 12:10 to find Richard dead and her life and her children's lives forever changed.

In the next few hours many people were involved and many things had to be dealt with. The shock created for Elizabeth a veil that blurred the sights and sounds of activity around her. When she recalled that time, she remembered everyone busying himself doing something purposeful while she sat there trying to breathe. That was the beginning of Elizabeth's isolation as the

3

wife of a suicide. Strangely enough, she did not feel like a widow.

The neighbours called the police, who removed the body. The police asked hundreds of questions and then told Elizabeth that an autopsy had to be performed and she would be notified by the coroner as to the cause of death. The cause of death? Elizabeth's first feeling of anger began, directed at the law for not allowing her choice about the autopsy and at the police for the inquisition they put her through.

A close friend gathered the children from school, and Elizabeth had to tell them. Since the body had been removed, the children were bewildered but were faced with visible signs of horror they had not witnessed. Elizabeth was blunt and told as much as she knew, but Peggy, age twelve, and John, age eight, each heard different things because of their confusion. Added to their shock was the pain of seeing their mother in tears.

Richard's parents, brother, and sister were notified and the family doctor and his employer were called. Each person who was notified asked the same questions to receive the same answers. WHAT HAPPENED?—SUICIDE. WHY?—I DON'T KNOW. Again, the beginning of a pattern.

For years this continued, lessening with time. Both the children remembered it differently. The circumstances of the death plagued the survivors. Peggy always remembered that she didn't kiss her father when she left for school that morning. For a long time John believed it was an accident—Dad was cleaning his gun.

Elizabeth and the children went through the ritual of the funeral, but that did not finalize the death. The grief and mourning were started and would be a longer and more difficult process than had he died from natural causes.

Often the bereaved, unable to answer the question Why? will begin to blame themselves and then others. Richard's parents never understood what happened. They gave him life and he chose to die. If only he had talked to them, told them what was bothering him. Maybe if they had gone over last Sunday he would have.... Then they made the assumption that the marriage was bad. If Elizabeth had been a better wife she would have picked up the clues.

Richard's brother Don blamed himself for not lending Richard money when he asked a year ago. To appease his guilt, he loaned Elizabeth money until the will was settled.

Janet, Richard's sister, blamed herself for pressuring him to be more successful, more like her. She had told him to cheer up when he got depressed. Janet also wondered if Elizabeth had been faithful and silently blamed Elizabeth.

Mr. Thomas, Richard's employer, accused himself of not being more aware that Richard's drinking was a problem. He pretended not to notice when Richard came to work with alcohol on his breath and wondered if talking to him would have helped.

Richard's death had sparked off the process of self-searching for many people. His friends and relatives faced the task of answering why he chose to die. This seemed to be unanswerable and is one of the worst frustrations to the bereaved. So everyone had his own theory as to "who is responsible," but they were not yet ready to talk about it.

Elizabeth had to spend the next period of time getting things financially settled. While the coroner's report was pending, the assets were frozen, and Elizabeth had to borrow money from the family until the will was settled. Once suicide was determined as the cause of death, Elizabeth was even in more difficulty. The life insurance policy did not provide for the family because Richard killed himself eighteen months after he insured himself, and the policy had a two-year clause. It was to be almost a year before the stipulations in the will were settled. But an even greater difficulty was that Elizabeth and her children would grope through an emotional jungle as the search began for answers to unanswerable questions.

Chapter II

THE FRAGMENTED FAMILY

*An odd by-product of my loss is that I'm aware of being an
embarrassment to everyone I meet. I see people, as they approach me,
trying to make up their minds whether they'll say something about it
or not. I hate it if they do, and if they don't.*

— C. S. Lewis
A Grief Observed

At the minute Richard shot himself in Toronto a young woman
died of an overdose in Montreal, a teenager hanged himself
in Salt Lake City, and a wife and mother jumped from a bridge in
San Francisco. That same day, throughout the United States, Canada,
and the rest of the world, people were destroying themselves.
Even though suicide death might seem like a solitary event, nothing could be further from the truth.

Suicide kills more people than all infectious diseases combined.
It is the fifth leading cause of death in Canada and the tenth in the
United States. Globally there are 1,000 suicide deaths a day (ac-
cording to the World Mental Health Statistics for 1980). Yet each
suicide death seems to the survivor to be an isolated phenomenon
and the bereaved feel alone with their unshared grief. For every
death, there are multiple victims, each of whom suffers for a long
time.

The ache of death does not end with the death of a person
(Feifel, 1977). Each person who survives the death of a loved one
experiences the loss as an agonizing and painful interlude to
living. The journey of grieving allows the bereaved to adjust to
living without that important person. When individuals are faced
with loss, especially death, they react with grief. Grief is an emotional response, the experience of a gamut of emotions that are
painful. Every person experiences different emotions at different
times and with different intensities. So, although everyone feels
the pain of loss, everyone expresses his grief differently. It takes

6

time to move through these emotions. One great difficulty in mourning death is the difference between society's expectations of the length of time it takes to grieve and the reality of the actual course of grief.

In a suicide death the time difference is even greater, that is, it takes even longer to complete grieving. The larger society becomes impatient. This is because there are added impediments to mourning a suicide death. One of these is the stigma attached to suicide. This stigma prevents the mourner from talking about his feelings, and that "talking about," the expressing, is the primary healer.

So, the loved ones of a suicide are left not only a legacy of grief but also a legacy of disgrace. This disgrace, this stigma, is unique to the survivors of a suicide death. In fact, the legacy of suicide usually combines stigma, guilt, and anger. This is what differentiates the mourning of a suicide death from any other death.

The stigma that the bereaved feel is imposed both from the outside by society and from within by their own feelings. The first agonizing shocks may be buffered by offers of support and warmth during the funeral ritual. However, once the funeral is over the surviving family members must face each other. As they do so, they begin to question themselves individually, each other, and society as a whole. While this is beginning, friends and other supports, reacting to their own emotions, pull back, and a form of isolation also begins.

Our society has standards, beliefs, and misinformation about suicide that stand as roadblocks to the bereaved's path of mourning. Society is offended by suicide death; our social mores condemn suicide. Suicide attempters keep their attempt secret. Suicide deaths are whispered about from behind closed doors. The whole subject of suicide remains a taboo of the twentieth century. Suicide is perhaps the only truly antisocial act. All others have socially satisfying resorts, ways society can punish the perpetrator of the act. In suicide a person leaves society, and society is unable to respond. And so, we (as members of society), leave those burdened by suicide death isolated and condemned, and we hope and pray it won't happen to anyone we know.

When Richard shot himself, the neighbours were a source of strength. They called the police, and after the body was removed they helped clean up. It was a horrible experience, but it needed to be done and they could at least do something. Then they helped with the phone calls that had to be made. So Elizabeth was spared these physical duties. The shock of the event and the duties being done by others produced an understandable separation from reality. But that separation from the activity around her grew and expanded into a feeling of isolation when the shock wore off.

Richard's parents insisted on paying for the funeral. It was their way of doing something, but to Elizabeth it signified rejection of her. She felt as if they were taking him away from her and negating her status as his wife. Because Richard's parents were searching for answers, they kept asking Elizabeth what had been going on. She could not answer them in any way that would satisfy them because she did not know why he made the choice to die. So it was impossible for her to talk to them about her questions and her feelings, and anger and blame on both sides prevented them from all sharing their sadness.

Friends began to insinuate that Richard must have been crazy. Elizabeth's silence confirmed it, her denial was seen as ignorance. Finally Elizabeth began to believe it herself. She told Richard's sister Janet, "I used to think suicide took sheer guts. I used to think you'd have to be brave, but now, all I can think of it is that he was crazy, mad, and in that state he killed himself."

When Elizabeth had to settle the finances she began to get angry with Richard. But who could she tell that to? Certainly not Don, Richard's brother, who was lending her money. Certainly not her children when she wanted them to have loving memories of their father. She wondered if Richard's boss had been giving him a hard time and blamed him. At the same time she knew Mr. Thomas was blaming her. She had heard him ask someone standing nearby at the funeral if Elizabeth had been running around. She could not talk to her children because she was sure they blamed her and could not have coped with their anger. When she tried to resume her old activities, she was regarded with speculation, with pretense (as if nothing had happened), or with implied accusations. So she stayed at home, feeling isolated from her family and condemned by the outside world.

There are obvious reasons for this societal banishment of survivors who are bereaved by suicide death. First, in North American culture, we are all fearful of death, especially death by suicide. We see death as the enemy and try to run from it. "In all of us," Herman Melville once wrote, "lodges the same fuel to light the same fire." We are all susceptible to losing the will to live, and at the same time when we see someone who has done just that, we panic. Will we be next? And second, we are unsure of the conditions and causes leading up to suicide and therefore have not figured out guaranteed preventative measures to protect ourselves and loved ones from this ultimate despair.

As individuals we fear death, we fear the unknown. We know our unconscious harbours self-destructive impulses that can occasionally emerge. Never having had to test our survival instinct in rigorous circumstances, we perhaps mistrust our ability to ward off despair.

Because we are afraid of death and because we are unsure of what causes suicide, we become fearful of contamination. If we can be contaminated in some obscure way by contact with survivors, we (as members of society) must isolate them, ostracizing as a way of keeping ourselves safe.

Perhaps we avoid survivors because they are a reminder that suicide can happen in any family.

Christianity cannot accept the sin of suicide, and for centuries organized religion has imposed hardships on the surviving family in various ways. Most commonly, the body has been treated in a punitive way. It is only relatively recently that in the Catholic view it is acceptable to bury the suicide victim in hallowed ground. In order to do this, suicide first had to be understood not as a sinful act but as the act committed by a mind not capable of knowing what he was doing: that is, at the moment of death, the suicide victim was insane.

In Orthodox Judaism also, the taboo on suicide was so great that a person who died by his own hand had to be buried in another part of the cemetery. The belief was that the physical remains might desecrate those buried near him. It is hard to alter a belief that has continued for so long. And so in life are those who bereave a suicide excluded from an important source of support.

In this social atmosphere the family develops a resistance system, a "them against us" barricade to try to protect itself from further pain.

Peggy was only twelve when her dad killed himself, and she still remembers this feeling of being trapped in her house:

"I can remember Mom looking out the window, watching the neighbours and saying she felt as if we had been quarantined. It really was like that. I'm not sure if we said 'Stay away' or if suicide repulsed everyone so much that they worried about being contaminated."

Our culture cannot understand suicide. It distorts our collective sense of purpose, shatters our beliefs in the value of life, and terrorizes our inner state of balance. To protect ourselves, we label the perpetrators of this crime against life as insane, while we try to figure out how to stop people from killing themselves.

"Bizarre methods of committing suicide, particularly because of the publicity they receive, are at least partly responsible for the still widespread view that all individuals who attempt, or commit suicide are mentally deranged" (Choron, 1972).

After a suicide death the survivors have to adjust to the shock not only that a loved one is dead but also that he might have been mentally ill. This is another of the many issues that the bereaved are faced with that impede healthy grieving. Loved ones often rationalize the moment of self-murder as temporary insanity while trying to understand the circumstances that brought about the decision to die. Society has always reacted to *craziness* with panic. Our greatest fear is dying; suicide death becomes through our fears an act committed by an irrational mind. This concern about the dead person's state of mind can affect anyone in the family: mate, parent, child, or sibling. As each person in the family tries to deal with these feelings, they often try to hide them from each other.

Suicide ignites our forgotten fears of going mad, of life presenting us with insurmountable problems. So after a suicide death, when the survivors are tormented by this fear that someone they loved was mentally ill, and when feelings of hopelessness emerge, they may themselves feel they are going insane.

Peggy recalls, "What really scared me most was that Dad hadn't acted crazy before he died, and then I thought . . . maybe it's because I'm crazy too; so I couldn't have noticed him."

Survivors often have had no preparation for the sudden shock, the horror. "The worst part," remembers Elizabeth, "was the suddenness and how to explain it. I felt everything was unreal, that I going crazy and that Richard and I were connected by insanity. It was as if we had this mutual flaw in our characters. He killed himself, but I'm the one who is still here—the crazy wife of the man who killed himself."

Sometimes well-intentioned outsiders intrude by commenting about the bereaved's state. Peggy's friends at school did not know how to broach the subject of her father's death and told her to act normal instead of crying so much.

"I guess no one knew how to treat me," she says now.

"I wish they could have just listened, but instead they kept telling me how bad I looked and how I was overreacting when some time had passed and I wasn't feeling better."

"I began to wonder what was wrong with me."

After a suicide death, some family members are left with a morbid expectation of the course of their own lives. Sometimes they wonder if suicide is inherited or they worry endlessly about others in their family killing themselves. John was eight when his father killed himself. As a twenty-year-old, his main concern right now is whether or not it is okay to have children.

"I guess I haven't worked out my feelings about it yet," he said.

"I've just always believed since it happened that I was born into a crazy family. I'm worried about having children; what would I do if they ever killed themselves?"

"What if my genes are filled with an insane wish to die. I don't believe that 'crazy' is 'curable.' That's what really scares me." It also frightens others. As a culture, we tend to scorn and stay away from craziness.

When the family members are grieving, they often go through such agonizing pain that they become suicidal themselves. If the surviving family member feels rejected, abandoned, lonely, isolated, fearful, and achingly sad, is it any wonder that he also feels suicidal? Since this may be a totally new and incomprehensible feeling, it gets confused with the fear they are also insane. Almost all survivors go through periods of feeling both crazy and suicidal, and they go through this horror alone. How can we tell our family, who is suffering so much from one suicide death, that we too are thinking of leaving them? How can we talk about our fear that we are going crazy, that we feel on the edge, when it is precisely the fear of insanity that is keeping our friends away and our souls tormented with doubt?

"After Richard died I was torn between wanting to end it all for me and wanting to live for the kids," remembers Elizabeth. "No one was very sympathetic to my crying—to my saying that I wanted to die too. They kept telling me to pull myself together."

But experts in this area of study know that those bereaved by suicide may be higher risks for suicide or suicide attempts themselves because the taboo has been broken in the family. That is, once a family member leads the way, suicide may become learned as the family's coping style. Survivors like John and Elizabeth need help in understanding that suicide can be the result of ineffective ways of coping with life's burdens and not an inheritance of insanity or suicidal traits.

Even so, the survivors often feel discriminated against, because they sense that their friends and neighbours have distanced themselves. They feel that the death has disgraced the family. These feelings of shame and humiliation can build up to such an extent that a family ends up isolating itself as a defence against condemnation.

Since society often condemns and ostracizes the survivors, it becomes difficult for them to make their way through the grieving process with much openness and support. If shame and stigma surround the mourners, they may feel inhibited in discussing the circumstances of the death. Some families feel that the suicide is such a disgrace that their intention is to prove to each other and the world that the death was an accident. By keeping the possibility of an accident alive, some family members never get the chance to deal with their true feelings. Excuses are made for the deception. Even if the circumstances of the death make any other explanation highly unlikely, family members may cling to one or another excuse to maintain the deception.

Richard's parents said, "We told everyone he had died of a heart attack. I didn't want the grandchildren treated weirdly."

"I liked being at home better than anything else for a long time after my Dad killed himself. I felt everyone knew and they were always talking about us (my family)," said Peggy.

As difficult as it is for the bereaved to work their way through the emotional mazes that block their way to feeling stronger, it is even more difficult for them if they set up the hurdles themselves. Denying that a death is suicide also denies the family members the means to work through some important feelings; the result can be confusion and despair for those needing openness.

There are other considerations as the family faces each other. Even though the family huddles together against the world and sets up barricades against intruders, this does not mean that the grieving process is taking place within the huddle. Family members often are unable to share their feelings with each other, so they in turn become isolated from each other. So the family member grieves alone and separately, not just because outsiders stay away from fear or embarrassment, but because he is not able to share feelings with those other sufferers whom he loves.

Each person looks at the rest of the family and asks himself, "Was I the most loved or most hated?" "Was I treated the worst or the best?" and he feels guilty no matter how he answers himself. These are subtle ways of realigning positions in the family. Of necessity, relationships must change when there is an absent member. When the relationships change, the power and control each member exerts on the others changes also. The power struggle may be to get closer to another person or to take more control over your own life and become less dependent on others. For example, if one sibling kills himself, one of the surviving brothers or sisters now becomes the source of strength and support for parents. When before he was not the favoured one, now he has attained a different position. Conversely, the unfavoured sibling may find himself with even less attention from the family. Or, if one parent dies, the child of the same sex may take on a parental role to replace the lost parent. There are many ways that the roles within the family will change, but these changes may come out of the early thoughts, "Who in the family has suffered the most?" and the quiet unshared individual answers.

They may also feel so responsible for the death or so angry with the deceased for having committed such an act that they end up imprisoning themselves, thus cutting themselves off from healthy interaction. In this confinement, they are unable to express their feelings and concerns and thereby start the healing process. Instead, their denied expressions of grief wound them further.

As Lindemann and Greer put it, "The survivors of a suicide are likely to get 'stuck' in their grieving and go on for years in a state of cold isolation" (Lindeman and Greer, 1953).

Sometimes there are people around to listen, but the bereaved feel that restraints are put on the kind of grieving that is permissible. It is a social practice that the dead are respected and well spoken of. Janet recalls how angry and bitter she was at her brother for killing himself, "I needed to rant and rave, to unload the anger that I felt, but no one would hear of it. I was told to pull myself together. It's strange but that was what I was trying to do."

Perhaps it is the anger, that basic crude emotion, that is the most difficult to express and the most piercing to hear, that locks so many survivors for years in their cold isolation. Even in families that share many private feelings, expressing anger at the deceased meets resistance. A parent may die by suicide and we often hear stories from children years later, when they have become adults, that it is still not permitted in their families to speak ill of the parent's decision to die. Anger at being abandoned by that parent is deflected. It is okay to blame doctors—anyone but the person who died. How can a child be furious with his parent if it wasn't his parent's fault?

It seems crucial to us that mourners have the chance to express their rage and anger. Oftentimes family members have tirelessly tried to help the person who ultimately killed himself. They can be weighed down by resentment when he dies, and they must first get rid of that feeling before they are able to begin living again.

Relief, especially if the relationship had become a burden, is a common feeling, and that compounds the guilt. Not only do some family members feel guilty because they were unable to help the deceased, but they feel resentful because they did try so hard to help. If we were resentful with the deceased for his behaviour, for his "refusal to feel better" before he died, we were likely to feel unable to express it then. This resentment may not disappear because one dies. Relief and resentment are the remnants of suicide, and we feel guilty if we experience them. Yelling and screaming, keeping journals, raging at pictures of the deceased, conversing with them in the dark, at night, as well as talking about it are all ways of dealing with the anger and make the rage more manageable and easier to live with. If families know that each member likely feels some anger, all will be free to express it.

Elizabeth found this prohibition to honest feeling especially painful. "For years I tried to help Richard, but he was always depressed, always wanting a way out instead of trying to change things. After he died, everywhere I went friends would say things like, 'He was such a fine man.' I always felt like screaming, 'No! He wasn't! He was depressed all the time and he made our lives miserable.' I always let the children say anything they wanted; they have their memories."

Allowing the survivors their memories is one way of helping them through the darkness. They need support and reassurance to be able to express feelings about themselves and feelings about the deceased.

"The worst thing for me was that no one mentioned Dick's name," said Janet, Richard's sister. "No one wanted to talk about him, and I was hurting so much—I needed to talk about me and him. I had the feeling he was forgotten as he died." Ironically, outsiders often refuse to mention the suicide victim's name. It is not that he was forgotten by those who knew him; it is as if he never existed at all.

Each member feels he cannot open up the subject for fear of making things worse. Everyone is shocked and hurt and the pain can be so intense that everyone is trying to protect himself and each other. Sometimes fears, anxieties, and guilt rage on in families for years. Someone in the family might feel they are held responsible because they were the last to see the suicide victim, or another family member might worry about being blamed because they had a huge fight with the person. Perhaps one of the main reasons some families evolve a myth about the death being accidental is because feeling abandoned is so difficult to live with. The family myth can be perpetuated for generations because the immediate family could not deal with the feelings of blame and abandonment.

Sam and his three children dealt with their wife's/mother's suicide this way, "We really didn't talk about her at all. In fact, we still don't. I was always afraid that the kids would blame me for Lyn's death, and I couldn't have coped with their accusations."

But the eldest daughter Joan has always kept her feelings secret because she remembers having a big row with her mother, "I was fifteen and wanted to go on this important date. She said I couldn't and I was very rude to her. I ran out of the house and the next thing I heard was that she was dead."

Joan still feels blamed by all the others in her family, "No one comes right out and says it, but I've always felt that my Dad and brothers blame me for my Mom's death. Mom and I never got along, and I think they believe I drove her to it."

The twelve-year-old says it another way, "My Dad said Mom shot herself accidentally, but it didn't make any sense because he blamed himself all the time."

Ed was fourteen when his Mom died, and the feeling of isolation took years to work out. "I really didn't trust anyone for a long time afterward. I always felt they would be friends until you needed them and then they wouldn't be around. I can still remember what it felt like to be left alone; my Dad and I had so much time —time to think, time to blame each other and ourselves. I really believe it would have helped to be able to talk to other people."

In this family, secrets have kept everyone apart; they still are not ready to share their memories and start new kinds of family interactions. Most survivors recall that period of isolation with sadness and years later still feel angry at being cut off from everyone else.

Explaining what has happened to children can be extremely difficult. But, children do not suffer emotional injury less because they are young. They must be told the truth so they can learn to trust both their own senses and the rest of the family. It is extremely important that they not be isolated within the family by secrets, especially because they are the ones most isolated by society. Friends and outsiders who come to comfort the adults usually ignore the children. Other children can be cruel and taunting, and the surviving child feels he has been branded forever for all the world to see. If he is feeling responsible (and likely he is), he needs plenty of opportunity to ask questions and talk about his fears and anger.

Suicide, more than any other family crisis, threatens the family and can produce maladjustments in individual members and the family as a whole. When supportive interaction is denied to some member, he has the added struggle of trying to make amends to the others.

So the stigma the bereaved feels comes from society's fear of contamination or fear of craziness or (as it is a reminder of mortality) fear of death. But those who are mourning also have fears—of inheriting suicide or insanity, of admitting to forbidden feelings or expressing them, and of continuing to be abandoned by those we love. So the mourner isolates himself, and this reinforces society's reasons for excluding him from the community. The circle of fear perpetuates itself.

It is the lack of supportive interaction following a suicide death that inhibits survivors from going through a normal grieving process. Social support has healing powers. "It is important for family and friends to discuss the death and its effects; mutual aid ensures for most people a relatively smooth transition from life *with* to life *without* the deceased. The grieving person and family are usually helped through such feelings as anger, guilt, and helplessness. The social network is quite important in influencing the process of bereavement (Solomon, 1981).

In some families these feelings, worries, and concerns are shared, but suicide has so many personal and social consequences for the survivors that in many families the horror and shame keep them apart in their private hell, hurting so much and yet unable to comfort each other.

There is neither a solution to the problem of living with grief nor a way to speed up the journey one travels while experiencing it. But it must be experienced; grief and all that it encompasses must be accepted. When we fight against it and try to get through it quickly, we become both impatient and angry with ourselves. When we put a time limit on our feelings and feel we have mourned long enough, even though we are not ready to stop, we run the risk of shutting down—of no longer talking and crying with others. If we allow society's expectations and ours to interfere with our own natural process, we may isolate ourselves. In a different way, and for a different reason—the stigma of mourning too long—we close off, and our mourning is incomplete. We need to remember that mourning a suicide death sometimes takes a long, long time. There are no quick exits; the road must be travelled.

What becomes apparent to the family members after a suicide death is the importance of each member being given the opportunity to share his concerns and fears. In an atmosphere of openness everyone has the chance to grieve at his own pace and also has the opportunity to raise issues as they become important. Certainly families could benefit from a support system outside the home where the bereaved could share their feelings without fear of being blamed or lectured. It is known that some families need the added support of other survivors who have experienced the same kind of loss. In this setting of mutual understanding, most are able to express concerns that have kept them from dealing with their loss.

Survivor-victims have a right not to be blamed or judged by society. It is important someday to be able to freely admit they are suicide survivors and that it is now part of their identity. The label *suicide survivor* focuses, not on the suicide, but on the survival. These people have come through their own public hell and survived (Hewitt, 1980).

BILBIOGRAPHY

Choron, Jacques: *Suicide*. New York, Charles Scribner's, 1972.

Feifel, Herman: *New Meanings of Death*. New York, Mcgraw-Hill Book Company, A Blakiston Publication, U.S.A., 1977.

Hewitt, John: *After Suicide*. Philadelphia, Westminster Publishing Company, 1980.

Lindemann, E., and Greer, I. M.: "A Study of Grief: Emotional Responses to Suicide." *Pastoral Psychology*. 1953, pp. 9–13.

Solomon, M.: Bereavement from Suicide (Research) Part 1. The Study in *Canadian Journal of Psychiatric Nursing* July/Sept., 1981, Vol. 22, p. 18–19.

Chapter III

"IF ONLY I·HAD . . ."

Wife at funeral: "I just can't understand why he did it."
Friend: "Don't worry, you're not to blame."

Old friend of family (in joking manner): "How's that crazy dad
of yours?"
Teen-aged son: "He's dead—he killed himself."
Friend: "I'm sorry. I didn't know; I didn't mean crazy."

Young daughter: "My mom said you wanted to see me."
Doctor: "I understand your father killed himself."
Daughter: "Yeah, he did."
Doctor: "Didn't anyone in your family notice him acting strangely?"

Husband: "Doctor, I just don't know how to go on living since Lila
killed herself."
Doctor: "Well, I just want you to know she didn't get the pills
from me."

Of the myriad feelings that surround a survivor, perhaps the most intense is guilt. Guilt defined as a "feeling of responsibility or remorse for some real or imagined offense or crime" creates questions of blame or fault. If we assume that the suicide death was an offense to both society and the family, we can presume that everyone connected in some way with the person who committed suicide will respond with some amount of guilt. Every person who kills himself had significant others in his life, and when he dies, we all wonder . . . Was I significant to his life? and consequently to his death? Even if we are not immediately concerned with guilt, society will do its best to ensure that we do concern ourselves.

Obviously the wife at the funeral, if not feeling guilty yet, eventually will as she gets blamed by others. The teen-aged son will wonder if Dad was crazy, and if so, feel guilty for not realizing and for not knowing what to do about it. The daughter will reflect on the

19

doctor's question and in turn question the family's responsibility. The husband is denied the help he needs because the doctor is wrapped up in his own guilt.

Guilt is an emotion that has so many different layers that it is perhaps the most difficult feeling with which the bereaved must cope. We blame ourselves not only for not helping but for all the earlier times we were not nicer to the person who died. We feel it is our fault because we were once angry with him. We feel as if we should have *been there* both emotionally and physically. The loneliness of the death is painful to us—we would not want to die alone. We also feel responsible for other family members to shield and protect them from our tears; so we either delay our anguish and pain, hide it, or go outside the family to express it. Then we feel guilty for not sharing it with the family because we are told it will make us closer. If we admit to a wide range of other sensations such as relief, anger, and liberation, we feel guilty for feeling those. We feel guilty because we were not a different kind of family with different values and a different life-style or because we did or did not live somewhere else. We continue to find reasons to blame ourselves, and each time we read something or step outside we have reason to believe society is also blaming us. So we fault ourselves for personal neglect (not caring enough), for ambivalence (sometimes hating), as well as specific instances of anger or hurt. We fault ourselves in the larger context for not interceding or approaching other significant others to intercede. We relate this to our not caring enough, but it probably has more to do with respecting privacy. We can say, "That's not my place," but it is hard to know what our "place" is, even in close relationships. So our feelings of responsibility demand that we look at the question of "Was it preventable?" We berate ourselves with "If only I had seen the clues, I could have helped." Possibly, but were clues given? Perhaps if we can assure ourselves that we could *not* have prevented the death, we can ease the awful burden of guilt.

First of all, we must remember that a suicide is always a choice, not one we would choose for someone we love, but a choice nonetheless. There are many choices in life that our children make that disappoint us, that our spouses make that anger us, and that our friends make that alienate us. But we must accept their choices and the feelings that those choices leave with us. The difference, of course, in the ultimate choice to end one's life is that it is irreversible.

"However impulsive the action and confused the motives, the moment when a man finally decides to take his own life, he achieves a certain temporary clarity. He also achieves some kind of minimal freedom — freedom to die in one's own way and in one's own time" (Alvarez, 1971).

One of the things the person who commits suicide may want is to make the people he leaves behind feel guilty. As a response to coping with *loss*, we have learned to feel guilty as part of our social conditioning. The suicidal death plugs into this soft spot we all have. So the person who kills himself knows that the pain he is feeling he can transfer to these others in the form of guilt. This may not be conscious realization, but it is based on a simple psychological truth. Every young child knows this when in anger he says, "If I die, you'll be sorry." The person who destroys himself either violently or nonviolently also wishes to leave behind permanent immortality; he will always be remembered in a unique way. His act is an irrevocable statement in which he rejects his family, and the family can never appropriately respond to that statement. So the suicide's act becomes family legend.

Still, we wonder if the chamber of loneliness could have been penetrated by someone determined and persistent enough, perhaps the warmth that seeped into that chamber could have helped turn despair towards hope. But we must remember that the person who commits suicide seals the chamber himself and rejects us. Having done so, he must now keep his intention secret. Once the decision is made, the anxiety appears to lessen, and the person appears to be coping better and be happier than before. The certainty of making a decision, combined with the possibility of transferring his pain (onto others) results in a lighter mood.

We have all heard stories of people who, after weeks or months of depression, suddenly get haircuts, take baths, leave the house, or pay their neglected bills days or hours before the suicide. One young man made his bed, cleaned up his room, shaved, and put on clean clothes. For two days he went job hunting. Of course his family was extremely relieved. On the third day, he jumped from a bridge. He left a note requesting that his clean clothes be given away.

Does this mean then, that if depression lifts it is a clue to suicide? It could be; it has happened before. But since it could also be genuine improvement due in part to the encouragement and support we have given those we love, it would be unnatural to assume that any positive change is really suicidal determination. How does someone become so determined to die that he insulates himself from his world and the people around it?

Adam was twenty-one when his seventeen-year-old brother Neil shot himself. Adam was away from home at school and had talked to Neil on the phone just two weeks before. They had made plans for Neil to go up and visit him for the Thanksgiving weekend.

Adam talks about his younger brother:

> It's almost as if he entered a tunnel that had to end in suicide. Once he entered that tunnel, no one could have reached him. He talked about the future, but he wrote about death and hid his writings. If he wasn't in that tunnel, maybe anything could have changed his decision—a game of touch football that afternoon, a kind word, a lot of homework. The only thing that relieves me of the responsibility is believing that he intended to commit suicide and nothing could have changed that. You either survive what comes up in your life or you don't. People deal with depressions, losses, etc., all the time—so I think that there is something—an x-factor, a fight, that was missing in Neil. It's easier to assume that he didn't have something needed to overcome these kind of setbacks than to assume these setbacks were the cause. This x-factor is not a thing but the lack of a thing—the ability to survive. Of course, if we believe there is an x-factor that is the cause, we can exonerate all survivors, because the suicide is inevitable. It is almost like predicting a terminal illness at birth. But I don't believe that either.
>
> What happens in your life may overwhelm you—for every human being there is an overwhelming point; therefore, everyone has a percentage of this x-factor. Some are suicidal in upper-middle class bliss, and some are fighters in the Holocaust. It depends on the amount or lack of an x-factor. I think the x-factor, the ability to survive, can be influenced at any time— any time before one enters that tunnel.
>
> I have to accept the responsibility for hurting him, but not for the taking of life—that's his responsibility.

It seems as if another reason the survivor searches for clues, then, is that if there were no clues, maybe it was an accident, a flirtation with death, a misadventure, but the intention was not to die. The authors believe, however, not that death came too soon through accident, foolishness, or whim, but that it came through deliberate, conscious, long-debated choices; a set of circumstances that culminated in an irreversible decision. That is not to say that this decision could not have been intruded upon and altered at an earlier stage, but when the person's focus becomes death instead of another way of living, it seems that all of his life's energies are directed towards that death.

From the authors' work with hundreds of people who have made suicide attempts and survived, they have deduced that this is different both in intention and action from the person who is determined to die. Someone who makes a gesture often does give overt clues beforehand and even more often calls for help immediately after injuring himself. His intention was to hope for help. He feels helpless but is still hopeful that someone else out there can do something to make him feel better. This is often seen as manipulation or attention-getting. He does need something and is asking for it; he is looking for a better way to live. If nothing changes, however, the ability and the will to survive weaken. He may then enter the tunnel that Adam talked about.

With the less determined, more ambivalent person, the clues or presuicidal communications that are given may range from blatant verbal clues to behaviour changes to a suicide attempt itself.

As early as 1959 a group of researchers looked at (Robins et al.) the extent and kinds of suicidal intent that had been communicated by talking to relatives of completed suicides. They found that only 60 percent of the people studied had given any kind of clue—but those that had communicated their intent had often done so as much as a year before the death, and the average number of communications of these people was approximately three (Lester and Lester, 1971). Most, therefore, do not leave useable clues of any kind. However, there are obvious statements that are made, such as, "I want to die" (not exactly a clue), "Life isn't worth it," or "You'll be better off without me." Why should someone say this if he did not want the person hearing it to stop him? He may have wanted to prepare his family and reduce the shock effect that they would eventually feel. He may have wanted to see if they care about him, to manipulate them to be different towards him in some way, or just to hurt and frighten those around him.

He may not really expect to be heard but will make statements that reflect his own thoughts and preoccupations. For any of these reasons he may state his intention and for many other reasons they are not heard. If the suicidal person is the kind of person who tends always to threaten or make exaggerated statements on other topics, it only seems natural that he would be viewed with incredulity and his statements with reservations and doubt. If the person has always been moody, his depression will be looked at as temporary and just another mood swing. But most importantly, when hearing someone you love threaten suicide, most people feel helpless. There may be anxiety, tension, and a wish to make the person feel better—but always helplessness. Out of this helplessness may come a denial, a refusal to accept the responsibility and, ultimately, guilt when the act occurs.

Sandra met her husband in college, and they married young. They had six children. His deterioration was gradual and extremely painful for the whole family. On looking back, she found no indication in those early years that her future would be so shattered. But after the children were born he started making threats of violence towards her and the children, which lasted for years. Eventually he began making suicide threats. Years before his death she began to notice erratic behaviour and frequent mood swings. They had gone for marital counselling, but he became violent before and after each session, so she refused to continue. He refused to seek psychiatric help until one morning he called his oldest son and asked him to take him to the hospital. Sandra remembers that morning when he told her he was going: "He came into the room and his hands were ice cold—I couldn't believe someone could be that cold and still be alive." He was admitted to a psychiatric ward of a hospital for a few weeks. When she visited him, he threw her out. He had made the decision to go to hospital but was angry with her because he blamed her for his being there. He was treated with antidepressants, diet, and exercise. Amazingly, at the end of three weeks the doctors told her, "We have not been able to help him, he's too glib, and there are people who are willing to cooperate who need the bed." Of this time she says, "I really don't think anything would have helped. He came home and spent the next three weeks mostly in bed with the covers over his head. I wasn't hoping anymore, I was just coping."

In spite of all the clues and all that Sandra was doing, she still felt helpless and that she was not doing enough. She stayed in the marriage, feeling it would keep him alive. Sandra had so thoroughly accepted the transfer of responsibility for his depression that in spite of all she did, she still felt ultimately helpless and guilty while he was alive, and long after his death. "What he left me was pain and suffering—before, he was in pain, I wasn't. Now he's free and I'll suffer for the rest of my life." In life he transferred responsibility for his depression; in death he transferred emotional pain. It is true that Sandra *felt* the responsibility and pain whether it was her husband's intention that she do so or not. We react to these situations in a pattern we have learned in childhood. Perhaps as a woman, she learned to respond as a victim, accepting responsibility when it was not hers. The pain is real.

Behaviour changes are often a clue that we might recognize as signs of suicidal thought, but often these changes occur slowly and we do not recognize them as a significant. Clues are most often recognized as real danger signals only in hindsight. All of us say things in anger or depression that are intended to hurt others. "I'll leave you" has probably been communicated in one form or another by all of us to loved ones sometime in our life. We may show our sadness and hurt in many ways, but only after someone kills himself can we say when we look back, "*That* was significant, that was a clue."

Most of us are aware of symptoms of depression—signals to us that the people we love or live with are behaving differently. We notice when someone has begun to withdraw from people, refuses to take care of himself, eats less, has difficulty sleeping, or begins to drink more. We might be concerned, but we might also hope it will pass, or feel it's just that he's overworked and look to time to alter the mood. What we all have more difficulty in recognizing, however, is masked depression. This is usually referred to when we talk about adolescents. When the depressed youth, unable to communicate his feelings, behaves in an aggressive and hostile way, we say he is *acting out* and needs controls. He is often seen as the typical rebellious teenager, acting in an unacceptable way, and so we punish him, ground him, or refuse him his allowance or the car.

On a larger scale, we may ask the schools or the courts to intervene and punish him for us. Often he does need limits and controls, and we do not know enough to look beyond his anger and see his depression. So what about the teenager who starts acting destructively with anger and violence towards others? What about the kid who skips school, shoplifts, starts using drugs, and destroys property? Don't all teenagers go through mood swings? Aren't there masked depressions that go unrecognized even by professionals? How can we expect ourselves to recognize these as clues?

So the survivor searches his own soul, takes inventory of his deeds, and sometimes finds that he must take a piece of the responsibility. But always, if honest with himself, the bereaved will remember that his loved one in the depths of despair made a choice.

Along with his choice to die, the person who killed himself may have made a choice to leave some message—often veiled, usually angry, and always desolate—in the form of a suicide note. While in life he may have felt he had no control over circumstances, in death he has found a way to control his family. Often the notes give directions requesting that the family carry out duties that the suicide victim felt unable to perform.

Sandra says, "One day I found a note on the kitchen table, and my daughter was very alarmed at the state of the handwriting. It said, 'I've got to get away for a couple of days, be in touch, Love, Ken.' Penny, our daughter, felt the note was ominous, but I brushed it off—I'd heard much of this, and it was like crying wolf. I thought, 'Oh, boy, here we go again!' He left the note at noon and shot himself at seven o'clock that evening in a hotel room. When he was found, so were several notes. There was one to me with instructions about the business, and one to each of our children. I gave the older children theirs; but the two youngest, not yet. The notes didn't help. They were faintly accusing and written in a state of insobriety or certainly a poor state of mind."

Another husband and father left a note to his wife requesting that she never tell the kids how he died. What a dilemma! She has to deal with them each year as they grow older, and they ask for more answers. She cannot, without guilt, share her feelings with them, as he imposed secrecy.

Sometimes there are other kinds of communications that come

to light later. Journals, poems, and school papers have often not been noticed and are then viewed afterwards as signs. One painful situation that occasionally comes to light is the letter written to a brother, sister, parent, or child before death that arrives long after the bereaved have been notified by the police that a loved one has killed himself. When the letter arrives, it seems impossible to believe the death has occurred. Not only does communication from the dead make the death unreal, but the letter itself appears to have clues, and so our guilt is enhanced.

Most notes, letters, or writings of any kind contain a combination of anger and hopelessness and are read, remembered, and kept locked away both in the drawer and in the mind. They do not seem to lessen guilt or make it easier to accept the death.

In any relationship innumerable things occur to cause anger, sadness, or guilt. We all share a responsibility for these. Is there a difference, then, in the guilt one feels once the person has left? In a suicide there is no way to share those feelings and so no fruitful way to address our stranded feelings of guilt.

Adam, who talked about his brother's death earlier, speaks, quite possibly, for all survivors:

> The hard thing for a survivor is accepting that the person is gone. It's as hard as an accidental death in terms of its suddenness and crueler because of its intention. Because it is sudden and cruel it really feels like abandonment. I had no chance to say goodbye, or to anticipate life without Neil, or to find out why *he* wanted to leave *me*. That left me connected to him even though he was gone. As survivors we feel angry as well as hurt by the person who kills himself. If there were clues perhaps you followed that natural tendency to back away, not get sucked in. It's important to protect yourself, too. But now that the person is dead, you feel responsible, and still connected to him with all your feelings. It's like the relationship is incomplete and you're left with an unanswerable reply—and until you end the conversation, you continue to search."

Our search for clues is motivated by our feelings of guilt and responsibility. This is a phase that we must leave behind as we go through bereavement. Perhaps this is what Adam means when he talks about ending the conversation.

No matter what we do or do not do, we will always feel guilty in the aftermath of a suicide. Maybe only time itself changes guilt into anger or remorse as we begin to realize that we in fact committed no crime—either through our behavior or our neglect.

We are rather the victim, left forever with a wellspring of sadness. But sadness is so much easier to bear than guilt.

BIBLIOGRAPHY

Alvarez, A.: *A Savage God: A Study of Suicide*. Des Plaines, Illinois, Bantam Books, 1971.

Lester, Gene, and Lester, David: *Suicide: The Gamble with Death*. Englewood Cliffs, New Jersey, Prentice-Hall, 1971.

Robins, E. et. al.: "The Communication of Suicidal Intent," *American Journal of Psychiatry* 115 (1959) pages 724–733.

Chapter IV

IF ONLY "THEY" HAD

After the bereaved blame themselves and become angry, they look around at the world and ask, "Could anyone have done something?" If we remember Richard's suicide, described in the first chapter of this book, we will also remember the confusion felt by each person who was close to him as they rocked between blaming themselves and anyone else who knew him.

Richard had been taking time off work or arriving late with alcohol on his breath. He often pretended to go to work, took his briefcase, said goodbye to the family, and went directly to a bar. Elizabeth felt Richard's employer should have called her, should have noticed something was wrong, and warned her. But communication is always a difficult process. His employer wondered if Richard was having marital problems, felt he could not intrude into his personal life, and hoped "things would get better."

Richard's daughter, Peggy, wondered if her dad was having trouble at work and why daddy's "mean boss" was not nicer to him. His son, too young to view the external world as being important and confused about the cause of death, blamed his mom. Why did she always fight with Dad? Maybe if she had been nicer to him he would not have been planning a hunting trip, and then he would not have been cleaning his gun. So Richard's family is typical of the private confusion each member sifts through as he tries to find someone to blame.

Anger is often the feeling that underlies blame. When we feel angry at ourselves, we also feel guilty and search for clues. We need to know if we really are guilty. As that anger shifts, as we begin to look outside ourselves, we condemn others, we blame others, and we wonder why they did not pick up clues.

The circle of blame often becomes a ripple expanding towards friends, school, church, or courts, depending on who might have had contact with the suicide victim. That anger often ends up focused on the professional helper.

If there are certain kinds of behavior that professionals recognize as high risk behavior—acts that might indeed be known to lead to suicide—and there are, why are not more signs recognized in time to intercept the pathway to suicide?

The authors do not know how many people who ultimately die by suicide have attempted suicide first and did not die, because record keeping is not standardized, psychological autopsies are not common, and many suicide attempts are never reported. In British Columbia, for example, there are a wide variety of categories of deaths that are reportable under Section nine of the Coroner's Act. This includes death by violence, misadventure, negligence, misconduct, malpractice, suicide, death "by unfair means," pre-or postpartum deaths, sudden or unexpected deaths, deaths from unknown causes while not under a physician's care, all prison deaths, and deaths from "any cause other than disease under circumstances that may require investigation." Despite the nearly all-inclusive nature of these categorizations, in practice roughly only one in five deaths in British Columbia eventually become coroner's cases. Therefore, somewhere between 70 percent to 80 percent of all death certificates are signed by physicians with no further investigation (Termansen and Peters, 1981).

The authors do know, however, by looking at recorded suicide attempts that were admitted to emergency wards of hospitals, and comparing those to coroner's lists of reported suicide deaths, that about 8 percent go on to kill themselves, while only 1.6 percent go on to kill themselves if they have received some form of counselling after the suicide attempt. In Vancouver during the five-year period between 1975 and 1979, there were 543 recorded suicide deaths. By checking those names with recorded suicide attempts during that same period we find that forty-one had made at least one previous attempt (Termansen and Peters, 1981).

The suicide attempt would then sometimes seem to be an indicator that this person is at risk to die by suicide in the future. Why then do so many suicide attempters not receive the offer of help that might prevent their ultimate successful suicide? Perhaps we have to look at those myths about suicide that confuse not only family and friends of the suicide attempter but many professionals as well.

"If he made a suicide attempt, he's just manipulative; he's not serious, so don't worry about it."

"If I talk to him about the suicide attempt, I'll just reinforce the behaviour."

"I'm sure he's learned his lesson and won't do that again."

"She just wanted attention."

"His grandfather often tried to kill himself—I guess it runs in his family."

"If she wants to die, that's her right, and I have no right to interfere."

Often the myths about suicide in our culture are believed by everyone. When believed by a professional helper, these myths collide with reality and override his ability to take a suicide attempt seriously. The following is an example of what might happen to a young person who makes a suicide attempt and ends up in an emergency ward of a major general hospital. When he is admitted to the emergency ward of the hospital, an intake sheet is filled out before treatment is initiated, unless it is impossible to obtain any information or unless he is in a medical crisis. In Vancouver, a form called the Emergency, Accident, or Short Stay Form will be filled out. There is a place on this form that says, "Nature of accident or Cause of injury" and another place for the final diagnosis upon discharge or before admitting to another part of the hospital. Since the youth is admitted to Emergency before a medical diagnosis has been made, the space for cause or nature of injury may say "*possible* overdose." Once a history has been taken, a medical examination taken, and the treatment performed, the final diagnosis will be written by the doctor authorizing discharge. However, the words *suicide attempt* will likely *not* be used as the final diagnosis. Instead, the chart might say: 1—personality disorder
2—drug abuse
3—situational reaction
4—suicidal gesture
5—adolescent adjustment reaction
6—manipulative gesture
7—juvenile delinquency

    8—accidental overdose

    9—chronic personality disorder

    10—suicidal gesture—no suicidal intent

    11—inappropriate behavior

Perhaps to say "suicide attempt" implies a judgement and is not a medical diagnosis, but how many of the preceding list are not judgements? The incongruency of the diagnosis with the information obtained from the history is the cause for concern. If the person is in emotional distress and has physically harmed himself, to say "suicide attempt" would usually ensure at least a psychiatric consultation and at best some kind of therapy that might prevent suicide. So a suicide attempt, if recognized as such, might have been a clue.

Another group of people, whom we can identify as being "at risk" to die by suicide, are those people who have been treated by a psychiatrist or have been hospitalized for a psychiatric problem. In the same study of 543 deaths over five years, 31.7 percent definitely had a psychiatric history. This does not mean that when a person kills himself he is crazy, or that he kills himself *because of the* psychiatric treatment. It does mean, however, that sometime during his life he had problems with living and may have sought help for those problems. Because he had more difficulty coping, he is more likely to give up. The "helpers" are not at fault for being unable to alter the ultimate end. An effort was made. We know the anxieties and self-doubts that professionals face when they become aware that someone they have professionally tried to help rejects and refuses life.

The excessive use of alcohol is often looked at later as a clue to suicide. One of the most prevalent assumptions today is that if someone kills himself, he was drunk—he did not know what he was doing or he needed the alcohol to give him the courage to perform the act. This is linked to the belief that people who abuse drugs and alcohol are slowly killing themselves. But in the same recent study of the people who killed themselves, only 28.7 percent had a measurable blood alcohol content upon death. This would support the authors' view that in most cases the decision to die was made with a clear head, the act carried out without a crutch, with the intention to die. Excessive use of alcohol may indicate problems with life but not the intention to end it.

Sometimes there are no clues, and sometimes we do not recognize them or ignore them because of our attitudes towards suicide. But all human beings want to postpone the inevitable darkness. We know we can die, but most of us, most of the time, tenaciously want to live. In our society we believe that life is a miracle and is precious. If we call the act of conception a miracle, the act of birth a miracle, then surely the act of living should be miraculous. It usually does not feel that way. It usually feels for most of us as if the act of living is a struggle—at times painful, at other times joyful. When joyful, we love life and fear our own death; when painful we feel anguished and hopeless. We battle with these painful feelings and gloss our image. But the suicide attempter touches a secret place in all of us. If we believe that we might be really incapable of happiness; we, too, might feel *that* angry and hopeless. The knowledge suddenly flashes that we can end the war ourselves. Those of us who witness suicide attempts want to deny that the varnish of a person's life can be wiped off by the act of living. We see through them our own fears and difficulties. So we may deny the suicide attempter himself.

So when we think the suicide victim's previous behavior gave clues to professionals or to people outside the family, that the suicide might have been imminent, we get angry. But just as we said in the last chapter, clues, even in the form of obvious behavior, are only *real* in hindsight. Myths and beliefs about suicide, personal feelings, and fears about life and death can hinder everyone's ability to predict suicide.

Feelings of rage, abandonment, and rejection leave the survivors with a new quest; before they were trying to fill someone else up with hope and self-esteem and feelings of self-worth; now they have the same mission for themselves. Anger can keep them from finding their road to recovery. Anger can erode their own sense of self-worth, their own reason for living, and anger turned inward also ends up feeling like burning guilt. This form of self-punishment cripples the survivor as he tries to make his way after the suicide death.

The anger the survivor feels when someone close to him dies by suicide has many facets. First he is angry at himself. He cannot

direct it at himself because he will either hurt himself or continue
to feel guilty. If feeling guilty or full of self-blame, he will not be
able to do anything that brings contentment or joy. His life becomes intolerable.

One way of dealing with the self-blame is to look at others and
become angry with them. So, anger at others is another type of
anger. This anger is one way for some survivors to live through
the tormenting pain at the beginning. If the anger festers, though,
it may be covered with a mask of tears. It is difficult for survivors
to choose between self-blame and the accusation of others. They
may end up in an unresolved and unbearable state of depression
and prolonged mourning.

Often a survivor will appear very sad and tearful. The sadness
is there—the loss and pain that is felt when losing someone close
is intense. Often the tears are also a mask for the anger and rage
locked inside. One woman told us that if she was not crying all
the time she would be screaming. "I know that there are a lot of
feelings locked inside me," she said, "but tears are my only way of
showing my pain."

For some people the exposure of intense anger or rage feels too
threatening and dangerous. "I know how those around me respond to my tears and sadness," she said, "but I'm not sure how
they would treat me if they knew how angry I felt." The authors
asked how she felt people would treat her, and what would happen?
She said, "No one would stay around. I would be left alone."

There is a third type of anger. The survivor may feel angry at
society because it didn't help his loved one. He is still unable to
appease his feelings because he gets no satisfaction when accusations are felt but not stated. Who can he yell at? He might write
letters to doctors, hospitals, courts, schools, teachers, or his friends.
There may have been real incompetence, but there is frustration
in trying to battle the *system*, not relief. Anyway, if the survivor
isolates himself even more by accusing others, he just ends up
with another reason for feeling angry. He is angry now because
society does not help him; it avoids him.

Sometimes the survivor may end up blaming the medical profession, mental health professional, agency, or institution unjustly.
But sometimes anger turned inward or not expressed can cause

real physical distress and hamper the survivor's chance to recover.

Physical illness seems to happen frequently to survivors, as does an increased number of accidents. It would seem to be related to emotional states, especially repressed anger. Sometimes the survivor feels frustrated that his own physical symptoms are getting worse, and many professionals do not recognize the relationship of this to the grieving process.

Hariet had been in severe *physical* discomfort since her twenty-year-old son killed himself. The authors asked her if she would like to contribute her experience by writing about it. Her reflections follow.

Seven months have elapsed since the tragic death of our son. Thinking back over those first dreadful weeks, I think of sitting on the beach in the quiet of the ocean where I could feel closer to Jason, yet the sorrow and emptiness churn within me. The majesty of the mountains in the distance seemed to signify the faith that God gave us. Beyond the mountains were the deep valleys of tears and despair. My thoughts rang out: "What a waste, Jason, why did you have to do it?"

A strong memory now is the intense heat of the August and September days. Heat wilts me at the best of times. It seemed that during those weeks my body was constantly damp, my cheeks flushed and burning, and my breathing irregular. I could feel my blood pressure rise as the day wore on. There was tightness in my chest and increased ringing in my ears. There was a constant feeling that I was suspended from a fine wire or that something was going to break or crumble within me. It was not until one day in October when I realized the feeling was no longer with me that I was really aware of how awful it had been.

During those early weeks everything seemed an effort. I was going through the motions of functioning, holding together; it seemed as though I was existing slightly removed from reality.

When I would go out somewhere, in a short period there would arise within me a feeling of panic; I had to get home. Or, if we were with people the conversation would seem futile, the time long; I just wanted to get home where I could let go, though once home I often couldn't feel anything. In a small room or sometimes in a group I would feel claustrophobic, a new experience for me.

My mind seemed to be in constant turmoil of the "ifs and whys" of Jason taking his life. I could not seem to shut out the thoughts. I felt hyper all the time, unable to relax, yet had a limited energy level. My husband and I found we had sudden outbursts of impatience or anger with each other.

During all these weeks I had not taken tranquilizers at all but required medication to sleep. As soon as I wakened, either during the night or early morning, my thoughts were on the subject, like a switch. When I don't take medication I seem not to sleep at all; it is like a dream filled surface sleep of brief intervals — it is the dreams that make me realize I do sleep.

Depression hung in the air. All day little things, letters, possessions, music, triggered thoughts. I would pray, play records, etc., to distract myself, only to have more thoughts burst forth.

I could not concentrate on reading, a favorite pastime. I reminded myself often that Jason made the decision to take his life, that he counted on us to understand. He seemed to communicate well with me and was close to me. Why couldn't I, his mother, on whom he most counted, why couldn't I accept and let go, let him rest in the peace that he sought? I tried to read a self-help book called *The Healing Mind* because I was putting such high expectations on myself to heal the grief.

Just before and at the time of Jason's death I was under medical treatment for hypertension and had to make regular visits to my doctor to check my blood pressure and adjust medication. I began to feel like a hypochondriac; it seemed each time I had a new symptom from heart palpitations, an irritating rash on my foot, or sharp pains in rib cage. Had my doctor even suggested to me that probably due to the emotional strain my body was reacting in its weakest areas, he would have eased my mind. Instead he was impersonal, seemed to be afraid of me, anxious to deal only with blood pressure and usher me out with "Come back in two weeks." Only once during these months since Jason's death did he ask me how I was doing.

Sometimes physical symptoms of bereavement are related to anger, sometimes to the pain of loss and loneliness. But the survivor will have another reason to be angry if the body's reaction to grief is not recognized. The unwillingness of physicians to deal directly with the patient's anxiety and feelings about the suicide death has been perceived by patients as rejection and disinterest. After a suicide death the survivor may go to the doctor's office feeling acute physical distress and really wish that the doctor will recognize the effect of the loss in their lives. For some patients the doctor-patient relationship is seen as the one place where the unmentionable would be safe to express.

"I wanted my doctor to say that it wasn't my fault that Jason had killed himself, but he remained silent about the death and I believed he blamed me for not doing more. After that I found it very hard being his patient."

Often the distraught patient will be handed a prescription for sleeping pills or tranquilizers and interpret this to mean that the doctor is reluctant to speak of the suicide. Though the doctor may have a discomfort about acknowledging the death, the patient may at this time lose faith that the doctor is someone to turn to and trust if things get worse. In fact, the authors were told of many instances where the attitudes of health personnel (social workers, doctors, counsellors, and psychiatrists) showed a reluctance to speak of the death or mention suicide to the survivor.

Often the survivor becomes embittered with the medical profession and does not seek out medical intervention when times become difficult and frightening. Sometimes rage and anger are displaced onto the whole medical profession, the survivor believing that the profession itself has failed them.

"Everyday people don't know such things. I thought psychiatrists were supposed to know how to help!" So the survivor experiences the anger at his own impotence, at fate, and at important people in his life.

Perhaps the most difficult type of anger to uncover is the anger at the suicide victim. Though painful to acknowledge, these feelings must be accepted before healthy grieving can take place. When the survivor first becomes aware, after the avalanche of feelings, that the one feeling that is really haunting him is anger, his first reaction is panic, "How could I be angry at someone I loved who is now dead? What kind of person am I, that I even get angry at dead loved ones? Am I going crazy? I will not admit these feelings to anyone!"

The anger gets clouded; irritation, bitterness and resentment also look like sadness at this time. The anger is buried along with the deceased, but the ghost of anger stalks the mourner. One survivor carried her anger everywhere, "Even if I was enjoying myself, I would remember what he had done, and I would forget about my pleasure and become filled with rage."

There is a cycle of anger and guilt that seems to spiral and interweave the emotional balance of the survivor. They feel anger at the dead person for leaving them, for the demand that the dead person made on them while alive, and at the sadness they are now left with. As they try to negate the anger and repress it into nonexistence, it surfaces again as raging guilt to torment their sense of worth. This in turn intensifies their anger at being dealt such an unfair blow, which in turn makes them feel guilty.

When the bereaved accepts the reality of the death, he is filled with impotent rage. But in searching for a place to put this rage, he is unable to find comfort. If he is angry at the lost one, he feels guilty; if angry at himself, he remains locked in despair. If he is angry at society and those people society deems helpers, such as psychiatrists, he denies himself the opportunity to share his grief with others who understand it and might be able to help.

Maybe one way of easing slowly into an acceptance of the death without blame is to look at how death must have appeared to the man or woman who made that choice, not how it appears to those left behind. If the suicide was viewed as an escape from a world that was no longer fulfilling, and seen as a peaceful alternative, not as a statement of blame or an accusation to those left behind, then perhaps we feel a little less bereft. Only then can one stop looking back in anger and begin looking forward to reassessing one's own life.

BIBLIOGRAPHY

Termansen, P. E., and Peters, R. W.: *The Certification of Suicides in B.C.* Health and Welfare Canada Task Force on Suicide, February 1981. (unpublished)

Chapter V

MY CHILD CHOSE DEATH

When you kill yourself, you not only shatter people's hearts, their
affection for you, their sense of responsibility towards you, you also
undermine their basic reason for living . . .
                                        —Françoise Sagan
                                        Scars on the Soul

Barb's son was fourteen when he fatally shot himself, and two
years later she still was not over the trauma. She had never
had the opportunity to grieve openly, and she was still full of
anger and pain. When the authors met her, she was one of thir-
teen people who showed up for their first suicide bereavement
workshop. They offered this supportive group experience to anyone who had lost someone close to them through suicide.

The authors introduced themselves and then explained how
they hoped this support would prove helpful. When everyone
seemed relaxed, they asked each person to introduce themselves
and share some pertinent information; who close to them had
died, the method used, and when the event had taken place.

Rather than reacting against such personal disclosure, everyone seemed ready to talk, and this openness proved to bring
everyone together quickly. Dr. Bruce Danto, a psychiatrist and
head of a Suicide Prevention Centre, relates that in his bereavement groups, "It is amazing and encouraging to see how quickly
strangers, whose common bond was the loss of a loved one through
suicide, formed deep and meaningful relationships. They all felt
at home immediately—as if wandering around in a desert for a
long time period before finally discovering an oasis" (Danto,
1977).

Within minutes of this group sharing, a woman whose husband
had killed himself reached out to Barb and said, "Any suicide

39

death is tragic, but to have your child choose death seems like the worst kind of hell."

Most of the members present nodded their heads in agreement. As Barb talked, the other group participants offered her their support as she struggled to make sense of her son's life and death.

Jeff was Barb's fourth child, her second son. "I remember the day he was born—how the sun shone into my room, welcoming the birth of my son. For a brief moment I understood the miracle of life—the warm rays of love glistening from me to my baby in my arms. I guess you always think that if you love your child enough, then your love will take care of everything.

Jeff was a rowdy and boisterous little boy who charmed everyone who came into contact with him. That was, until he went to school. Even in kindergarten the teachers had trouble with him. He was disruptive in class, he had a poor attention span, and he was unable to do some of the simple tasks that others his age could do. By grade two, when all the other children were learning to read, he was still having difficulty with the alphabet.

"Through the years we tried everything," Barb continued. "We changed schools, we went to all sorts of doctors, we tried everything we could. Most of the professionals said he was just lazy or not disciplined enough. I always blamed myself for his problems. I knew he was clever, but I couldn't figure out why he couldn't learn or wasn't interested in school. He was always meeting failure and always getting into trouble. No one ever mentioned learning disabilities—they always implied that if we were more effective as parents, his problems would go away."

"Then, when he was ten, my husband and I separated. I knew that this was a very difficult time for Jeff, but I was hurting also, so I don't think I helped him too much. I tried talking to him about his Dad's leaving, but he always shut me out. He rarely saw his father after that. I knew he was hurting, but I couldn't do anything about it."

"At around age twelve we hit a whole new batch of problems. Now he wasn't confining his mischief to school and the schoolyard —that year he got into trouble with the police. It started with shoplifting and destroying public property, and then when he was fourteen he stole a car to go joyriding. Throughout this whole period I was really in a panic. I tried every recourse possible: school counsellors, psychologists, psychiatrists, probation officers. Once I even pleaded with the judge to put him in an assessment unit for delinquent teenagers. He was out after one week because his assessment read, "Jeff has some family problems, but is a normal teenager with a healthy outlook on life." He killed himself two months later.

"I'm still angry at the authorities, at the justice system that didn't offer any treatment, and at myself for not screaming louder. I blame myself for his death, because I worked when he was small, because I stayed in a bad marriage for so long, because I divorced his father. The list is so long; sometimes I can't remember one thing that I feel proud of, that I think I did well. . . . "

Barb felt very alone after Jeff's death.

"I always felt like screaming, but I didn't. I just kept silent and carried the pain around."

Barb had friends and her other children and relatives around, but no one felt comfortable talking about death or about Jeff.

"I was confused before he died; after he was gone, nothing made any sense."

"I couldn't figure out what I believed in any more."

Suicide seems so worthy of blame by all of us; other deaths are perceived as lying outside one's control. Death by accident or disease seems inevitable—it happens regardless of one's actions. But, suicide seems preventable. Culturally we expect to lose our elders, but when our youth die, we also lose our goals and our hope.

"When your parent dies, you have lost your past. When your child dies, you have lost your future" (Sarnoff-Schiff, 1977).

Parents of a suicide often feel shame compounded with grief, especially since parents are supposed to help a child grow and to protect and keep him from harm. A child's death seems an unutterable waste. For the parents the resulting anguish and pain are devastating.

For Barb's life to have any meaning, she first needed to work through her feelings of inadequacy, her anger at professionals, and her anger at Jeff. She had blamed herself for so long for Jeff's death that this self-imposed judgement kept her from renewing her interest in living. Dr. Danto says that:

"Along with feelings of guilt, there is an unconscious resentment towards having been electively and publicly abandoned by a son or daughter who, in the minds of parents, catastrophically showed that their love was not enough. Most of the parents who have come to our group admit that they are burdened by this feeling of being a failure" (Danto, 1977).

"It's a feeling of failure and also powerlessness" adds Barb.

"There is nothing I can do to change what happened, but I keep going over and over the same territory, trying to find another reason to blame myself. Where did I go wrong? How did I fail? And everyday I can find a new answer. I can remember every mistake I made for fourteen years."

But no matter where the discussion takes these parents, as they open up to their feelings of family and shame and guilt, the word anger rarely comes up. When anger is revealed it is often directed towards themselves and others in the community (psychiatrists, nursing staff, the justice system), but rarely at their child for taking his own life. Perhaps, since it is socially unacceptable to talk ill of the dead, they would rather not blame the deceased or admit to tortuous feelings. When asked about these feelings of anger, Barb said, "It's scarier to be angry at Jeff than at myself; it's too overwhelming, too dark to think anything negative about him."

As Barb talked and felt understanding from the rest of the group, she became increasingly prepared to explore feelings; she realized what had kept her from being angry at Jeff, "For a long time I felt Jeff's suicide was like a banner advertising my ultimate failure as a parent. That was bad enough. When I did realize I was angry, I was not able to admit that I was angry at my dead son. Even when he was alive I had trouble sharing my angry feelings about him to others; that always felt wrong. So after he died I tried to control those feelings until I ended up feeling numb."

Although parents directly experience the pain when adolescents commit suicide, our whole culture reacts to adolescent suicide. We are puzzled by it, and angry that our youth should reject what we as adults are offering them. We also offer them other more appropriate ways of dealing with pain or confusion, and they reject our solutions too. When an adolescent kills himself, adults want to scream, "But he hadn't even started to live yet!" His life was so brief; the tragedy is enormous.

Suicide is the second highest cause of death among adolescents, surpassed only by accidents. As a result, adolescent suicide has been an area of concern and has been a special field of study for the past several years. Adolescents are swamped by emotions as they try to figure out the world and their relationship to it. They blame themselves for the disorganization, the highs and the lows, and the frenzied search for concrete answers. Their lives are often a difficult puzzle, and the pieces do not yet fit together.

What problems at this age seem so insurmountable that they feel desperate and suicidal? The best known contemporary expert, Edwin Schneidman, says that, "Every case of overt self-destruction is better understood as an escape from rather than a going toward" and suggests that the most common emotion in suicidal crisis is not hostility but despair" (Schneidman, 1970).

Suicide might sound like "I abandon you," when really the adolescent might have been saying, "I abandon pain."

Adolescent impatience and turmoil cannot always hear the adult commentary on life: "Wait until tomorrow, it will get better." "This is not so important—you'll understand when you're older."

For some teenagers the only reality is anxiety; the challenge presented by living becomes anguish. In order to mask their depression, adolescents often show others marked mood swings, aggression, and maladjustment or acting out. These behaviours are seen as rebellious or infantile ones, which will be outgrown.

An American study by George Masterson found that anxiety and depression were common in ordinary adolescents. Inner turmoil, self-deprecation, and ideas of being laughed at are all common. These feelings cause appreciable personal suffering to the adolescent at the time but usually do not last and are unnoticed by adults.

Erik Erikson has described adolescence as the period in which the main psychological task is to establish a personal identity. This is an awesome chore for a person to work through in the midst of clashes and conflicts. All of a sudden adolescents demand independence and support while they often rebel against guidance and control. They often protest the quality of a parent-child relationship and yet detach themselves when parental concern and interest are demonstrated.

"I knew Jeff was hurting—sometimes he was lethargic and depressed. I tried everything I knew to help him through, but he never opened up to me. His last words to me were: 'You don't understand.'"

Most adolescent suicides who left notes felt their problems to be insurmountable and felt they could not be helped. Madison suggests that most of them probably knew their act would result in death: "It is not a last desperate call for help, but a statement about life and death" (Madison, 1978).

Barb: "I remember I once told Jeff to face reality—his Dad wasn't going to change and become more available. His note said: 'I am facing reality.'"

Jacques Choron asks the question whether it is possible that at the moment when human beings become capable of starting their own lives they have a tendency to refuse to do so. He also states that the adolescent is particularly prone to overstep the boundary between a thought and its execution. The adolescent questions himself and the world, and he is often acutely preoccupied with death in general, his own death and suicide (Choron, 1972). Many of us will remember as adolescents such preoccupations.

When parents of children who commit suicide are involved with other survivors—because they can give voice to their questions—they have the opportunity to do the investigative work, going over the same territory to find some answers to try to understand the reason for the suicide. For Barb the search led to a greater understanding of adolescent depression and suicide; others in the group shared how their dead teenagers had dealt with crises or how they remembered those difficult times. Slowly Barb was able to understand Jeff a bit better, "I'll never really know all the answers, but I don't feel so boxed in anymore. At least I've been able to start remembering Jeff as he was—the sadness is still here and probably always will be, but I'm not so afraid anymore, especially of me and my feelings."

Connie is the mother of a thirty-year-old daughter who killed herself with carbon monoxide exhaust from her car. Connie was a single parent and Kim her only child. Kim's death left Connie not only bereft of her child but also of her role as mother. Where once she had been both a wife and a mother and had been able to fulfill herself by nurturing, now she had been robbed of a special role and one of her reasons for living.

Kim had been a bright child who always did well in school but who had high expectations of herself. No matter how well she did at anything, she felt it was never good enough. She was constantly disappointed in herself, and she and Connie had talked about this often. They were close—mother and daughter—even after Kim married. Kim had done well in school and had done well in her job. But at the time she was offered a promotion she became depressed, convinced she could never handle the added responsibilities. Perhaps she entered marriage as a solution; a job she could handle well. But the perfectionist child was one who had not socialized easily. She had grown into an adult who could not relate intimately because she would not allow herself to express to anyone what she considered negative feelings. If she felt trapped in the marriage, if she felt anger at her situation, she did not tell Connie. Connie will never know why Kim killed herself when it looked as if life was just opening up to her. Connie suspects Kim may not have been able to have children, and for someone like Kim that could have been disasterous. Connie will never know for sure and what she torments herself with is, "Whatever it was, why didn't she talk to me about it?" The pain of losing a child is not less because that child was now an adult. That child was the baby who needed a parent and the adolescent who needed that parent to help him separate from his home. But the task of being a parent will continue. Separation is never expected to be sudden, complete, and final, as it is in death.

For parents like Barb and Connie, for all the other fathers and mothers whom the authors have met, the greatest help and relief came from being able to explore their feelings about themselves and their children who had died. The dead must be allowed to die before the bereaved will be able to illuminate and consolidate their own lives.

For married couples living together after the death of a child, the grieving process can get *stuck* by one partner trying to treat the other. Sometimes the wife will show her sadness while trying to coax her husband to open up about his feelings. There is no special way to grieve, no rules that have to be followed, no time frame that must be adhered to. Each person in a couple must find their own pace, allowing each the freedom to go as fast or as slow as is necessary. Sometimes being in a supportive group helps; each parent is able to go their own distance and get support from others. It is very difficult to get support all the time from someone who is hurting greatly too. So often it is heard at group meetings that each partner was afraid to open up about their hurt feelings because of fear that the other mate would become depressed.

Will and Lee came to a support group one year after their seventeen-year-old son had hanged himself. They were experiencing anger and guilt but not talking about it.

"We talk about his having made a bad decision, but I can't imagine screaming at Don for killing himself; instead we sometimes scream at each other and make ourselves feel worse," Lee said. Their relationship was suffering, their pain was still acute, and the tragic death still loomed over their lives. Instead of being a mutual support system for each other, their grief distanced them from each other. Will blamed himself for Don's death, but he wasn't able to express these feelings and didn't feel comfortable showing his emotions. "Sometimes I feel Lee doesn't believe I'm as sad or hurt as she is. But I'm crying on the inside." And Lee felt she had to control her emotions in front of Will: "I can always sense that my tears frighten him—I feel he pulls away from me when I cry, and then the loneliness is unbearable." Others in the group were able to share their experiences and feelings with them. Sometimes only one of a couple will come to a group meeting, but even these parents go away feeling better understood and supported. Sometimes the members of a marital couple are split into two separate groups, so they will be less inhibited. This was done with Will and Lee. "My biggest problem in grieving was my loneliness," said Lee, who felt particularly alone, "because my husband blames himself so much for our son's death that he doesn't like to mention his name. At least here I can talk about Don, and I'm beginning to understand that Will needs to grieve in his own way."

Barb had to go through a long and difficult process before she began feeling better. Others in the group were very supportive.

The interaction always allowed each participant to expose their feelings without the threat of ridicule or judgements being made. Barb was able to talk about her feelings of failure as a wife and a mother. She was able to admit to past mistakes and realize that she had made some important valid decisions in the past. Assured of the group's support, she began remembering Jeff's life and became aware that there was a lot she had forgotten about him.

"Before I came here I never mentioned his name. I was always afraid that no one could understand my pain—all I ever thought about was how he died. I forgot to remember the living Jeff. So I guess I wasn't grieving his death and dealing with my loss; instead I was stuck at how he died and I just couldn't get past that by myself."

This is a common barrier to the grieving process for many, and sometimes they truly need the assurance from others that it's all right to go further back, to a time before the death and the circumstances of the suicide, to be able to start coping with their loss. Especially important for parents whose children have died is the need to remember and cherish these times. They have given so much. For example, Barb needed to remind herself of the time Jeff fell when he was five years old, hit his forehead on an end table, and had to be taken to emergency for stitches. She remembered how he held on to her and how much love and comfort she gave him. She also remembered how the two of them used to joke about it after, she teasing him that it was lucky he had a scar or he would be too good-looking when he grew up. The bond between them had been there. She had not been a terrible mother.

The group was a safe place to talk about the "whys?," the "where did I go wrong?," the soul searching that most parents who lose children have to go through. "I'm beginning to realize that I'll never get over Jeff's death. It will never feel okay that he died that way, but slowly I'm learning that as I become freer to think about him and cherish those memories, it becomes less scary to let myself go, to think about him, care about him, and miss him. I'm not afraid anymore that my emotions will strangle me or that I'll crack up."

When the group first came together, it was acknowledged that losing a child through suicide was one of the most devastating horrors to face. But, because everyone was mourning, Barb knew that she was in a safe place and would not be rushed or pushed.

"Somehow when I first realized I was in a room filled with people who had suffered a loss in the same way that I had, and that they understood that I was in excruciating pain, somehow I relaxed, just a bit, but enough to take my first breath in a long time. I remember thinking, 'I can breathe. I'm not going to suffocate." That's how it had felt for so long . . . like I was going to choke, that my emotions were going to kill me."

"Another amazing thing happened when I was so free to talk about Jeff. I realized that so many people never mentioned his name at all—it was as if he had never been born, had never cried and laughed and brought us both sorrow and joy—had never *been* alive. So I had needed to hold on to all the pain as a way of holding on to his memory. I had needed to remind myself in some way that I had had a son, because everyone else was denying it."

"But I remember that people in the group cried together at that first meeting and we laughed together too. I started to believe that maybe I could be helped and that I could help others too. I had forgotten that others hurt too. We never really found out why each of our loved ones had killed themselves, even though for a long time each of us asked the same question over and over: "Why?" "What could we have done to stop them from dying?" I don't remember when, but after a few meetings the questions about suicide stopped, and I think we started to explore how we could begin to live again. There was much more room to go when that question was asked. Sure, often times the pain and the guilt and the horror would surface again, but I already had a taste of feeling better, so each time I felt a little stronger or maybe a little surer that my pain would subside again and not control my whole being like it had before I was part of the group."

"Sure, I'm still angry at the authorities, at all the professionals who didn't know enough or didn't care enough to help Jeff. And I'm still angry at Jeff's father for not showing our son the love and attention he deserved and wanted. And I'm still angry at myself for the mistakes I made, but I don't hate myself anymore. I don't feel that I'm an awful person or that I was such a bad mother and that is why he killed himself. And I've learned to let go of my anger instead of letting it entangle me and make me feel resentful and bitter. Now I allow myself to think back, back to what we did have together and about my life now. I'm more able to talk about it now. I don't panic if his name is mentioned and I don't punish myself anymore with the "What if's." Another thing that's changed —I don't hide myself on important occasions and bear the hurt alone. Jeff's birthday, the anniversary of his death, the start of a new school year, or even a change in seasons will bring memories flooding back. Almost anything can remind me of him, and I used to cry alone. Now I try to talk about him, and it does help. For a long time, everytime I saw someone his age, I would see him. That's diminishing now and I can bear to be around young people again."

When Barb was asked what else might help her, she said she wanted to help other people who were bereaved by suicide. She eventually had that opportunity.

"I had a need to have some purpose come from his meaningless death. So, I agreed to share my story in the hopes that others who had experienced similar pain would feel less alone. I've been interviewed by the media twice now; the newspaper and radio. Neither time was Jeff's suicide sensationalized, and it felt good to think that possibly someone who was hurting as much as I was might be comforted. My biggest hope was that someone who was mourning might feel ready to reach out to whoever would listen because I had been able to talk openly about it."

BIBLIOGRAPHY

Choron, J.: *Suicide*. New York, Charles Scribner's, 1972.

Danto, B. L.: *Suicide and Bereavement*. New York, MSS Information Corporation, 1977. (Edited by A. H. Kutsher)

Madison, A.: *Suicide and Young People*. New York, Houghton Mifflin/Clarion Books, 1978.

Sarnoff-Schiff, H.: *The Bereaved Parent*. New York, Crown Publishers Inc., 1977.

Schneidman, E. S.: *The Psychology of Suicide*. New York, Jason Aronson, Inc., 1970.

Chapter VI

RUPTURES IN THE RELATIONSHIP

Where Do I go From Here?
Tell me, where do I go from here?
You said you'd take me through
  the years,
So where do I go from here?

It's colder now
Trees are bare and nights are long
Can't get warm since you've been gone
Can't stop singing sad songs.

Lovers' plans,
Like fallen leaves on windy days,
Flutter past and they fly away.
I thought I knew you oh so well,

And I need you now.
I need to feel you in the night.
I need your smile so warm and bright.
I wish my mind could let you go.

Where do I go from here?
Tell me, where do I go from here?
You said you'd take me through the years,
So where do I go from here?

Words & Music—Parker McGee, 1978.

Poignant enough is the music of today, when we listen to songs of lost love with the ears of someone needing comfort, and how much more meaningful is that music if we listen with the soul of a survivor. The music speaks eloquently for the husband or wife whose spouse has killed himself, and it helps voice the pain and longing of the one left alive and perhaps even soothes him. Music has always done this. But for how long, how many years, must one seek solace for an act that took only minutes to perform? What about the marriage vow, " 'Til death do us part," when even in death the marriage lives because the spouse's way of dying haunts the house they shared. Death is usually both an ending and a beginning. But if there is a suicide death in a marital relationship, this is not so. The actual ending of the relationship lingers long after the ending of life. That is the process of any bereavement, but in a suicide death the remaining spouse grieves longer and more painfully and in his or her own mind remains a spouse long after the act of death.

A marriage may begin to die long before the suicide death of a spouse. As previously mentioned, someone who kills himself was both angry and hopeless. What is it like to live daily with someone who is depressed, angry, and hopeless? What does this attitude towards life do to his behaviour, and how does that in turn affect the caring and communication in the relationship? The depression has caused the individual to withdraw or behave differently. He may feel like a burden and in turn act like one. The usual method of communication between the partners has changed or doesn't exist at all. Often the suicidal spouse is so changed that he is already lost to those around him long before his actual death.

In one study of the time of death, college students were asked to choose one of seven alternatives as the circumstances under which a person is considered to be dead. The seven choices are as follows:

1—when he first learns he is going to die.
2—when he first enters a hospital knowing he will never leave.
3—when he first enters a nursing home knowing he will never leave.
4—when he loses self-awareness.
5—when he becomes very senile.
6—when he wants to die or gives up on life.
7—when his heart stops beating.

Only half the students used the biological criterion of cessation of heartbeats as the event that signified death. The others used psychological criterion instead. Thirty-five percent said wanting to die or giving up on life indicated death (Lester and Lester, 1971). So it seems that the person who kills himself may not only have felt dead for a long time but may have appeared dead to those around him.

Sandra, whose husband had been depressed for years before his death, said, "Grieving had begun in a gradual way so far back, his suicide was a quick excision. Living with him had been like having a block of cement tied to your ankles, and it was so hard to stay afloat. His actual death was not a tragedy; the tragedy happened long ago, when he began to fall apart. He was a great brooding presence in the house. He sat staring into space towards the end. We couldn't laugh or even speak. Within two or three days after his death, I said, 'It's progress of a sort,' because we could begin to breathe, we could begin to live again, we were in control. 'Thank God, we're safe!' "

When Sandra talked about her marriage and how it had broken down long ago, the authors began to wonder how often the marital situation is bad at the time of death and if this in fact influences the suicidal act. They found some interesting and valuable reports while searching the written material available and from talking with spouses who had been married and some who had been separated at the time of the suicide death.

Samuel Wallace wrote a book about twelve women whose husbands committed suicide at about the same time in which he looked at the influence of the "marital relationship" on the suicidal act and the effect of that act on the widowed survivors. In five of the twelve marriages the men needed special care, due to physical handicap, alcohol problem, of some kind before their marriage, and all five of the women knew that they would have to fulfill these needs before they married their husbands. Therefore, in these marriages, the need *for* care joined with a need *to* care. In the other seven marriages the men also needed special care, but this need manifested itself after marriage—for example, disabling work accidents. The more care the wives gave, the more the husbands seemed to need, so the wives took over all responsibilities. Along with this there seemed to be a kind of deception, one that grows out of lack of communication between partners about the pattern their marriage has taken. At the same time, an isolation from outside help occurred. In this silence sex life deteriorated for all. At this point some began to reverse the pattern of care, responsibility, deception, and isolation. Four of the wives left their husbands, two spent long periods elsewhere, and one emotionally separated. This was the beginning of the "death" of each for the other. Before, they fantasized things would get better; now, they fantasized things would get worse, and to meet that expectation they did. The spouse's indifference to whether the relationship continues is communicated to the suicidal one. He experiences himself as being invited to stop living, and he obliges. So it appears that suicidal men may be protected from suicide by the marriage, and when an emotionally overloaded marriage breaks down, the suicide occurs. In other cases the husbands' physical or mental disorders had severely interfered in the marital relationship so that the marriage had socially and emotionally disintegrated (Wallace, 1973).

Husbands who are surviving spouses do not as readily talk about their marriage problems and do not go to "helpers" as frequently. The authors believe that for men the most severe kind of loss that leads to depression is a loss of self-esteem. For women the most difficult loss is the breakdown of a relationship. Widowers have been heard to say over and over, "Why couldn't she have told me—why did she keep what she was feeling from me?" So it does seem as if the communication has also broken down in marriages where the wife is suicidal. For the woman that may have meant the relationship itself had broken down. Thus she felt an extreme sense of loss, which leads to depression and suicide.

It would seem that it has been a socially and emotionally dying marriage when it ends in suicide for the husband. The authors believe that this is also the condition of the marriage when it is the wife who kills herself. The men who talk to us speak of their own failures in life and tend to paint pictures of healthy marriages. They see their failures in relation to their jobs and even their children but are confused as to what happened in the marriage.

Society judges the loss of a spouse as more terrible for the survivor if they were living together. Separation or divorce suggests the end of mutual caring, and often these survivors are not supported by family and friends. But whether married or divorced, all must go back and look at the relationship as it once was before going forward to a new life.

Laura's husband had left her, at her insistence, several months before he hanged himself. He had been drunk and abusive throughout their marriage. However, especially in the early years, she felt sorry for him because of his unpleasant childhood and wanted to "make it up to him." When his violence became worse, she finally persuaded him to leave and refused to allow him back. For months he begged and pleaded or harrassed her. He threatened suicide many times, and the day of his death he called and begged once again. She says she felt mostly pity by that time but was determined to protect herself and her two children both physically and emotionally. His death, however, did not mean he stopped living for Laura and her children. He remained alive for years in ways that sometimes made her wonder if she was going crazy. She would feel him watching her at times, would waken in the middle of the night and see him standing at the foot of the bed. She would see his face flash before her at unexpected times, often when she was with another man. She would hear his voice begging her to forgive him. These visions and voices became especially vivid and frequent on the occasion of an anniversary that they normally would have shared—his birthday, or the kids' birthdays, or their wedding anniversary. The anniversary of his death always has special meaning for her. The visions became even more real when she began to make a new life for herself, so that she felt she had to ask his permission for anything she wished to do. Sandra, too, felt her husband return to her and watch her and her children at the kitchen table. She, too, remembered special times and anniversaries with distorted pictures of her husband's face in front of her.

These two women, one physically separated, one living with her husband but emotionally separated, experienced their husbands' deaths in similar ways. It appears not to matter whether one is married or separated or even divorced when a suicide death occurs. The fact is that when two people are emotionally tied, suicide leaves one dead, the other heavily burdened and often emotionally dead for a long time. In a marriage, the depression of one partner so erodes and gnaws at the relationship that when the rupture comes many feelings are released, one of which is relief. But the feeling of relief is personally unacceptable, because death by one's own hand is socially unacceptable. Now those left behind are left with many feelings that are unacceptable about oneself. It matters little whether the deceased partner was loved or hated, fought with or endured, cared for or neglected. He was once loved and so felt to be special, thought to have valuable and admirable traits, and now the survivor must question his own judgement. He must also question whether he is lovable. "After all," the thought must go, "if I was lovable, wouldn't those who loved me want to be with me?" The survivor becomes disillusioned with love, distrustful of human relationships, and perhaps the worst feeling of all starts to bubble inside—low self-esteem. He sees himself as deserted, abandoned, and therefore worthless. The death is an implicit statement that the spouse was unable to "make him happy" and was therefore partially responsible for the others desolation. Guilt, anger, and low self-esteem are a dangerous combination. All of us must sometimes resist the desire to escape the daily struggle of life. We push away the feeling of futility and the temptation to slide into a warm and peaceful nothingness. But if our spouse, who we at one time loved and admired, yielded to that temptation, then we become more ready to consider it ourselves, for ourselves. Especially because we feel unlovable now, the daily struggle seems less rewarding. We are angry, too, and so we may turn this hostility upon ourselves and see the appropriateness of our own death.

How can one cope with these feelings, diminish the pain, gradually begin to smile, and eventually to laugh again? How can the spouse accept responsibility in equal measure for the relationship up to the end and still understand that she is *not* responsible for the suicide? This is so important and yet so difficult to grasp. Many people cope in ways that prolong the grief. They may deny the fact that it was a suicide or call it a noble gesture, or alternatively tell themselves that the suicide victim was ruthless and condemn him as a "bad person." We feel it is healthier to see the suicide act as a deliberate rejection of the world and of the human relationships in it. Survivors need to see this but they also need to see that they can still be good and loving, not destructive people. Some see loneliness as intolerable and so become frantic in their activities or become preoccupied with helping others. Both activity and concern for others are important steps in taking control over one's own life again but should be balanced with other responsibilities, rest, play, and fun.

Others, feeling helpless and unable to have any effect on life's events (because of an inability to help the partner) often feel unable to make their own lives purposeful or meaningful. If one is able to talk openly about the rage and impotence, the loss and loneliness, a normal period of mourning can occur. But surviving spouses now have all the problems of a single parent, usually without other family support. If the in-laws are not avoiding the now needy spouse, they are probably blaming her.

"My in-laws won't even speak to me, and I thought they really loved me."

"His parents lied to the children about how he died; now I have to deal with their suspicions."

"I'm afraid my in-laws will turn the kids against me—they've never forgiven me for Sid's death."

"I go over there for the sake of the children, but I always feel their anger towards me."

"They had him for twenty-three years; I only had him for three—so how could it be my fault?"

"Where's their compassion—if they had been more forgiving maybe he wouldn't have been so depressed."

On, on, and on, over and over, frustration and anger are voiced at the rejection felt by survivors who thought they had been loved and find they have lost not only their spouse but his family as well.

So much has been written about the damage that the suicide does to the survivor that it would be easy to conclude that all survivors not only suffer significantly but also grieve forever. It is thought that by understanding the influences that affect the mourning process and by expressing and sharing the feelings that accompany it, the grieving can be shortened and life can be seen as challenging and purposeful for the survivor. Also, it is believed that even without guidance from others some survivors successfully adapt and find ways of coping with a suicide in a healthy manner.

Just as the music of today speaks beautifully of the survivor's feelings, and "Where do I go from here" might indeed be the common question all surviving spouses might ask, no one can speak as movingly as one who has experienced the loss of a husband or wife. Sandra found that writing her feelings in the form of poetry helped her face her loss and in her dialogue with her dead husband we feel her anguish but also see her move through pain towards acceptance and hope for her future and that of her children. She does not need to hold on to her grief to hold on to his memory.

But the process is slow. As we read the poetry, we see the same feelings emerge repetitively until they somewhat alter with time, and human resilience takes over. This steplike process is symbolic of the timing of the grief process itself.

October 6th, 1976
5:45 AM

You're gone
And I don't grieve
Your living death
Is done.

You were everything
In life to me . . .
But you began to die
So long ago.

We who love you
Now remain
And we shall live
To glorify
What once was you.

Doubt not
My love and gratitude
For happy times
In time
Just those
Will persevere
And through them
You . . .

October 10th, 1976

Why is it birds chirp
And firm their winter plans
Just at the moment
We plant you prematurely
In the very ground
      Which feeds these winged ones?

Don't fret, my love—
For finally you're at one
With things . . .
And to a number
We shall celebrate your peace.

And we will carry on
To dignify the memory
Of a man
We'll always love.

October 27th, 1976

Desperate
You dealt out
Fire and brimstone
To all around
Who loved you.
And we burned and hurt
And agonized—
Oh how we cared!

With so much fire
To hurl about
How dreadful
Must have been
Your own inferno!

But you've gone Home
And all your hurting
Now is done.
And we who love you
Celebrate your peace.

And soon, we too
Will find a haven of a sort
From hurt.
Tough canvas covering
Spots once soft and open
And receptive

Fire cauterizes too
And we'll emerge
More flint-like
For our wounds.

And when God's healing
Is complete
Our minds will just discard
The harsh realities of "now"
And all that shall remain
Will just be Love
And joy and gratitude
That you were once with us

Exuberant
And full of fun
Your brief but vital
Life . . .
Ago . . .

November 4th, 1976

We met
And loved
And planned our life
Together

We forged our plans
And children came
And troubles came
But so did joys
And we walked through them all
Together

Somehow, the more we faced
The greater was our joy
In one another
We two could whip the world
And then sit back
And chuckle over things
Together . . .

Just when
Did you begin to loathe
The products of our lives
Together?
Just when
Were children competition
And not friends?

Just when did I become
Your competition too
And not your friend?

It's lonely where I am
For you are gone ...
And by your own design
You've chosen to wipe out
"Together" ... forever

Rememberance Day
November 11, 1976

I've just passed through
A long, black tunnel
of despair
Missing you until I thought
My soul might split

It didn't though ...
Just nearly
You almost did me in
In your despair

But I've survived
And start to see
A chink of light
Towards the other end.

I'm sound of mind and soul
And body
And so reject
The sad, accusing, tragic aspect
Of your farewell to us.

November 12th, 1976

Where did things go wrong?
Just when did you begin
To loathe and to resent
The plans we made together?

When all we hoped for
Was a family
Forged by our love
For one another ...

Their health and beauty
And potential
So far exceeded
Our wildest hopes.

These half dozen
Masterpieces
Resulted from our love ...
Just we two, — and God, of course

I'm glad you left me them
Exquisite and just so full
Of talent, character, and hope
For a life —
I wish you could have known with them

My heart and soul,
My very life ... aches
With loneliness for you ...
Who helped me make them happen.
Having made them happen
You found
You had to leave ...
I understand.

They are in good hands
And I shall carry on
As I feel you'd
Have me do.

Rest in peace,
Sure in the knowledge
That I <u>will</u> care
For yours and mine
As I know
You'd want me to.

New Year's Eve 1976 to 1977

You took your life
And lashed at me
From your selected grave . . .

I take the shot
And don't resent . . .
It was your plan
As such—I must accept it
And I do.

I shrink and weep and shudder
The solitude I feel
Just almost crushes me
And yet . . . not quite . . .

I'll rise above this all
And yours and mine
Will recognize
And maybe even celebrate
The love—which made
It all begin.

Early January 1977

I'm glad that you are resting . . .
In life you so loved your bed
And blankets overhead—
And sweet oblivion—
Eternal rest for you must be truly
Heaven.

Rest for me has always been
The last resort . . .
Just something to be gotten through
The better to get on with Life
Refreshed, restored and strengthened
By its healing balm.

January 14th, 1977

Why then—oh why?
Do you persist in the tormenting
Of this, my necessity in life?
Do you not know that I am
Having to be
Both you and me?
Not for me . . .
Or even you
But just for "ours"

You've gained your rest
Please leave me mine!
I need it to survive . . .
And fill our dual roles

January 31st, 1977

I've been away—
I've just come back
Your absence screams at me
From every corner
Of the home we shared.

But busy now
With your affairs
And mine
And ours . . .

Screams soften
And become
An omnipresent murmur
One day the murmur too
Will die
And I shall learn to live
With silence.

BIBLIOGRAPHY

Lester, Gene, and Lester, David: *Suicide: The Gamble with Death*. Englewood Cliffs, New Jersey, Prentice-Hall, 1971.
Wallace, Samuel: *After Suicide*. New York, John Wiley and Sons, 1973.

Chapter VII

DAD—WE'RE HALF A FAMILY NOW

You don't mean what you say
You don't know what you know
You don't feel what you feel

—Adele Faber & Elaine Mazlish
Liberated Parents/Liberated Children

Children of suicides are often kept in the dark about the events of their parent's death. Secrecy and deception are apt to hide the children in a confusing world of emotions. Those important people in their lives may believe the children are being protected from despair and pain. The darkness usually frightens the children more as they learn that the adults are not wanting them to know what they know and to feel what they feel.

The authors met a family similar to Richard's family. The father had chosen the same way to die, and the children were even younger than John and Peggy. The biggest difference between the two situations was that in this case Ivy, the mother, did not want the children to know the circumstances of their father's death. She felt that they were too young and fragile to comprehend his final decision. She believed that her two children, Tommy, aged six, and Jan, aged ten, had enough of a loss and tragedy in their lives learning to live without their Dad. So, the storyline was fabricated to protect the innocent; Dad had been cleaning his gun and it had accidentally backfired and killed him. At the beginning Ivy's struggle was difficult. She needed time to adjust to her husband's death and she needed to sort out her feelings about his decision to die. She needed time to heal her emotional injuries. She was sensitive and vulnerable and believed she was in some way implicated in his death. Her grieving at this stage took her through a maze of uncertainty and confusion. In this exhausted state she struggled to hold herself up—to keep afloat and not be drowned by emotions.

Her purpose now was to console the children, to protect them from further pain, and to save them from more hurt. Later she would recall, "I think I might have hurt myself if it had not been for the children. My main concern was taking care of them and not letting anyone else hurt them. Bert had chosen to die, but I didn't want the kids to know. I thought it would affect the way they felt about me, and themselves, and certainly the way they remembered Bert."

The result was a barrier set up, with the world on one side and Ivy and the children on the other side. Not only friends, neighbours, and relatives were pushed away, but so was the reality of Bert's death, as Ivy tried to protect the children. She and the children would be safe as long as no one from the outside intruded and shook up their safe world.

"I kept everyone away, feeling that they might intrude by discussing Bert's death. I felt a bit safer, a bit more in control, if I kept other people away. Then maybe I could save the children from the pain that Bert's death brought me. Keeping them safe became my only goal."

But the children's world was already filled with unknown horrors. Their dad was dead, they were confused and hurt, and their safety net had snapped. Tommy referred to his family as "half a family" now, and no amount of silence and protection would change the truth that his dad was gone. Although Ivy believed she could save the children from greater pain, the veil of secrecy did not protect them from experiencing guilt, anger, and sadness in relation to their dad's death.

Eda Le Shan, in her book *Learning to Say Goodbye*, notes that, "Children often experience their own horrors after a death. Aside from the specific incidents prior to the suicide, the children often feel they were primarily responsible for the general background events and feelings that led to suicide. That is, the child was convinced it was his basic badness or his father's disappointment in him that bred unhappiness and ultimately suicide. Or, he blamed himself for a good share of the marriage difficulties—for consistently siding against the suicidal parent in arguments" (Le Shan, 1976).

Often a child will be aware of previous suicide attempts or threats. He may have agreed to keep these occurrences secret or ignored them because he felt helpless. He may have witnessed quarrels between the parents and heard his name mentioned. He often will feel responsible, especially if he remembers times when he misbehaved.

All children, no matter what age, sense the tragedy and feel confused. They can see who is weeping and who is no longer at home. If the missing parent's disappearance is not explained in a way that satisfies what they already know and feel, they will be extremely confused.

Ivy had no way of knowing that Tommy blamed himself, that he had a recurring dream that his dad was angry at him. He had heard relatives after the funeral say, "He couldn't take it anymore," and, "The pressures were too great," and he remembered making his dad angry the day before and now thought that he had caused his Dad's death. He did not have any real ideas about suicide, but the information he did receive was contradictory, and this confused him and isolated him since he did not feel safe to question his mom. Years later, when Tommy was fourteen and knew more of the facts about the suicide of his father, he still blamed himself for arguments that he remembered were about him when his parents fought. This sense of guilt had to be explored and resolved in Tommy's adolescence before he would be free to live without the anxiety and self-blame.

Jan, at ten, had a little more understanding about suicide. Though Ivy never admitted to Bert's choice, Jan had enough awareness to know that it was quite unlikely that her dad had been cleaning his gun. He had never even mentioned a gun, and she couldn't figure out what he would have used one for. But even more burdensome for her was the knowledge that he had been drinking heavily. She had come home from school early the day before he shot himself and had found him drunk and distraught. She had promised him she would not tell Ivy. Now she lived with the agony of blaming herself for not getting help for him, and though her mom insisted Bert had not been depressed, she had her own ideas and no one to share them with.

The suffering does not begin for a child after a parent has killed himself. Often the child has lived through years of strife in which both parents have shared their lives with an incompatible spouse. Sometimes a parent has been depressed for years before the final suicide act, and the child has lived on the edge of guilt for a long time.

In a family where there has been marital warfare, the child might have been targeted as the problem. After the suicide death of a parent the powerless child might view himself as the cause of death. In the other parent's confusion and anger, he may also focus on the child as the problem. The surviving parent might openly accuse the child of being one of the reasons for the death.

Experts have observed that it is the ability to check out facts that allows a child to believe what has happened. But limiting a child's experience by not letting him know the truth can confuse his sense of reality and his trust in himself to observe correctly.

Most children of parent-suicides who were studied by researchers were found to largely distrust the reality of their experiences. These studies have shown that the inability to accept reality seemed to be related to a prolonged, confused twisting of the truth around their parent's suicide.

Even though a parent may honestly believe that the child has no information about a suicide having been committed, parents must realize that the child will have heard, seen, or felt something unique. This discrepancy forces the child to try to make sense of the situation with limited access to more information. Unlike an adult, a child will take the conflicting messages personally and include himself in any imagined blame.

Children tend to think the memory of the dead parent belongs only to them. *If only I had* becomes the focus of all their thoughts, and their self-blame becomes enormous. They cannot bounce back and forth between blaming themselves and others as adults do, because they believe *they* were the most important influence in the parent's choice.

Ivy spun the tale; the children tried to follow the storyline. The tale did not allow for elaboration or for pauses that were long enough for the children to inject their questions. It did not provide an arena where the children could discuss their concerns and fears about their father's death and the circumstances of death.

There was no place to add that they were scared, that they blamed themselves, and that they did not understand what had happened. They had not yet reached maturity, they did not yet have enough understanding of the complicated issues involved in a choice to commit suicide. Their experiences limited their view of the dark world of a suicide victim's choice. Pretending that their father had not killed himself was a complicated way to deal with a situation that was filled with unsuspecting snags—they were told one thing (that it had been an accident) and yet were treated another way. Ivy dreaded talking about Bert for fear that she would show her anger or express her own sense of guilt, and so she actually shut the children off from some important feelings. Since the most important part of living through a terrible experience is to understand and accept the feelings about the experience, it becomes evident how a family myth can keep the children of suicides lost in their own world of prolonged misery. Here the child is so overwhelmed by intense feelings, so confused and scared by inner turmoil and conflict, that he is unable to express his true feelings. The healing that must take place for any person who has lost an important person in his life never really begins until the loss is recognized and dealt with and the feelings accepted and acknowledged.

But if the parent died by accident, why does everyone act as if he had done something wrong? Along with tears, children will sense the anger.

For Ivy, Bert's death was a hostile act and, though she would much later recognize his death as an antidote against his own pain, her anger seethed just below the surface, and the children were silenced by this threat of rage.

Another type of conflict can arise: the surviving parent talks to everyone, especially the children, as if the partner who died was a totally marvellous spouse, parent, and human being. He becomes idolized and worshiped. But the children remember the bad times and wonder if one has to die to be considered good. If *they* are bad, will *they* be remembered as good? This may be the start of the belief that some children carry with them forever. It can grow and become a conviction. An example of the idea is that, "Inevitably, when I am a certain age and at a certain time, I too will die by suicide. If I fail at something, if life should ever become intolerable,

I can escape, and I will be remembered as if I had always been good."

The authors have talked to many children of suicides who as adults continue to struggle with the fear that they will commit suicide. For Jan, the tormenting thoughts of her dad's death plagued her through her adolescent years. She believed he had killed himself (although her mother always denied this), and she had a quiet fear that she would lose control and kill herself too. Sometimes she thought about killing herself to join him, and other times she felt she was losing control and would not be able to stop in time. When Jan was asked if she had even mentioned this thought to her Mom, she was shocked and said that her mother did not allow the word *suicide* to be mentioned in the house.

Children are alerted if the adults in their lives seem afraid and unsure. When a parent shows that he is in a vulnerable situation, the child's sense of security may be threatened and the child will try every means to reestablish the parents' sense of safety. After a suicide death, when the adults feel so victimized and confused about the reality of a mate choosing to die, the children are left to their own resources to deal with their fears and concerns.

A very young child will try desperately to bring back the parent. Several incidents have occurred of young children dressing up in the dead parent's clothes. Another way a child may do this is to try and take the absent parent's place in the family. If Mom has killed herself, the daughter may do many of the household chores and assume much of the mother's role and responsibilities. Initially this is comforting to the rest of the family and helps her feel good. But growing up suddenly can quickly become a burden. The young son tries to be a source of strength and protection for his mom and may even be told, "You're the man in the family now." What happens to this "man" when he needs to cry?

Jan was ten when her dad died, and she had stored up memories of how life was before that fatal day. After the funeral she noticed a widening gulf between her mother and her grandparents. Now there was little opportunity for her to be with them in any meaningful way. Bert's parents blamed Ivy for not being a more attentive wife and not taking better care of their son. Ivy did not want her children influenced by their grandparents' attitudes, and more than that, she did not want them discussing Bert's decision with the children. And so the visits between Jan and her grandparents lessened, and Jan had to live with this loss, too. Experts who have dealt with some children of suicide victims have witnessed that many of these children received messages that they should not know about the suicide and above all should not tell anyone about it if they do know. The implied threat is that it is dangerous to know and tell of these things.

If grandparents and other relatives are not invited to share important events because reminders of the past are too painful or because of fear that the truth will be exposed, the children lose a great deal. Grandparents are a source of love for the child at a time when he especially needs to be reminded that he is loveable. But they also are the link of that child's personal heritage, between generations, and reminders that he had a long line of ancestors and that life goes on. The family itself must not eliminate opportunities to discuss the trauma. Clear communication of reality between grandparents, parents, and children can prevent the stunting of emotional growth in the children.

The distortions of communication can leave the child feeling remote and incapable of effective action. Tommy could not describe his feelings at this stage, but his behavior attested to his fear concerning any learning in school. He could not trust what he knew to be true and grew timid about receiving information in general. Cain observed this phenomenon in his work with these children: "In many cases knowing becomes dangerous only as related to suicide, but in others it spread to learning and knowing in general, and played a major role in learning disabilities and conditions of pseudostupidity which emerged after the suicide" (Cain, 1972). Tommy told his teacher he did not understand the work more and more frequently after the suicide. His teacher mentioned that he never offered his opinion anymore, and Tommy replied, "I have none."

Mental health professionals agree that traumatic experiences in childhood can arrest emotional development, and since the suicide death in families is often hidden or denied, children often have trouble relating external events to their inner thoughts, wishes, and feelings. What can happen, therefore, as a result, is that suicide is experienced in a highly personal way as abandonment and rejection, reinforcing feelings of worthlessness. Throughout Jan's teens she had to struggle with the normal alienation and self-esteem problems of adolescence. "But I always felt bad about myself. My Dad hadn't loved me enough to want to stay with me, so I couldn't have been important to him, or special as a person in his eyes. So who could ever see me that way?"

When these children grow up, they often have great difficulty in forming intimate relationships. It has been difficult for them to trust their own feelings because of the confusion around the reality of the death (what they know on a feeling level was denied). It is also very difficult for them to trust those close to them because of the fear that they will leave or lie to them. If others cannot be trusted because of a fear of being left, if feelings cannot be shared because they are not believable, how can lasting, intimate relationships be formed?

All children who had a parent commit suicide are not doomed to suffer bleak, insecure, and confused adulthoods. The grown-ups can be helpful if they understand what is needed. Understanding the child's behaviour is an important first step. We can know that the child also goes first through a stage of denial, of disbelief. But a child may pretend it is not happening. He may refuse to talk about it at this time as a way of refusing to allow it to be true. He may play pretend games with or about the missing parent.

A child may suddenly exhibit unusual physical symptoms or illness. He may act angry at others in the family or exhibit delinquent behaviour at school. Children often act out their feelings rather than expressing them. The behaviour may be misinterpreted. If the young person is fearful, it may be related to helplessness. So he acts as if he is in control all the time. He may be filled with rage and direct his anger at everyone. But his anger may only be a refusal to agree with your perception of what happened.

"Two of the most painful days for children are the birthday of the deceased and the anniversary of the suicide. Continue to observe them; don't pretend they are ordinary days" (Hewitt, 1980).

When the denial and anger stop, there will be much open grieving. As adults we need to help the young person—of any age—talk about blame and responsibility. We need to remind them that, "No one knows what goes on in the heart and mind of a person before suicide. What we perceive as self-murder may be an act of loving self-sacrifice" (Hewitt, 1980).

Let them see your tears and know that it is desirable to express grief. Talk about the deceased as he or she really was. Reassure the child that you will not choose to leave. Above all, listen carefully. They have questions, just as you do. But you need to allow them to express their questions; answer those you can and share with them the pain of the fact that many questions will never be answered.

Share their concerns. Take into account the age of the child, and make your explanation simple. Admit that the parent chose to die because he was in too much emotional pain or too much conflict.

Perhaps when truths are told and hurt is shared, respect and love of survivors for each other can surface. Now it becomes important to discuss better ways than suicide to handle problems. Out of the pain the child can indeed grow.

BIBLIOGRAPHY

Cain, A. C. Ed.: *Survivors of Suicide*. Springfield, Illinois, Thomas, 1972.
Hewitt, J.: *After Suicide*. Philadelphia, Westminster Publishing Company, 1980.
Le Shan, Eda.: *Learning to Say Goodbye*. New York, Macmillan, 1976.

Chapter VIII

MY BROTHER, MY FRIEND

Adam did not come for help in grieving his brother's suicide. He came because he was experiencing a different crisis—the breakup of his marriage. But as his immediate feelings of loss and pain of separation were explored, the grief feelings about his brother emerged. This earlier loss had occurred years before, but the old memories and feelings about his suicide came back with a fresh intensity. Through discussion one of the authors and he came to understand many things once they made the connection between his past loss and his present crisis. The timing, as it happened, was right. The author had already become interested in understanding and working with people bereaving a suicide death as an extension of her work with suicidal people. She had just completed her first survivor group. In working together with Adam she saw clearly how unresolved grieving weakens one's ability to cope with future loss.

When the authors began to write, it seemed important to bring Adam's brother Neil to life in these pages and at the same time refine from his image more general qualities that could serve as illumination to all who come in contact with teen-agers. Neil was, after all, seventeen years old when he took his life, and Adam knew him well. Better, in fact, than anyone else, though not well enough. We talk about the teen-age years being difficult times, we say the task of adolescence is to separate and become individuals unique from parents, and we say teen-age suicide is on the rise. All of these things are true, but what is also true is that we really do not ever *know* other human beings; we cannot get inside their skin, view their world, and experience their pain. So, to ask Adam to tell us who Neil was and why he killed himself is to ask him to guess, to ask him to continue to search into history, and to ask him to stay in that time period. Of course this would hinder Adam's progress. Instead, with Adam's help and his poetry an attempt will be made to transcribe what he as a surviving brother went through in the hope that others will benefit from his experience.

Adam:

I have something to say:
Exactly one year ago I was deep in an annual contemplation of fall and the significance and approach of winter. I wrote two poems in the midafternoon dealing with the sacrifice and/or suicide of life in the face of an awesome, indefinite, perhaps eternal winter, and the potency of the magic that lies in the uncertainty there.

Magic Sam and Jimi Hendrix were dead. Janis Joplin was either dead or soon to die. Everywhere people would talk about how, in our culture, this was the time that dying took the stage.

Then the phone rang.

My father had a very poor connection. He said something had happened to a member of the family. I could feel my face get hot; I asked who. He said, "Neil is dead . . . can you fill in the rest?"

I envisioned him fallen in a construction pit or in a car accident. I had no idea what my father was asking me. Just three days earlier I'd talked with Neil on the phone about his decision to go to a school to become a forest ranger and about him coming out to stay with me for a few days at Thanksgiving.

Then Dad said Neil had shot himself with the .32. Now I pictured Neil dead in the basement.

He asked me to come home right away—mother and he needed me immediately.

I called Don, and without telling him anything asked him to drive me to the airport. I walked to the Student Co-op and borrowed enough money for fare to New York. I couldn't speak to Don all the way to the terminal. Then I could tell him. He embraced me.

My father met me at Kennedy, where I told him I'd be arriving. He had an overcoat on and was smoking a cigar. I saw him at the bottom of an escalator. He held out his arms and we hugged each other long and hard.

He told me it had happened in Neil's and my room. He told me about the music on loud up in the room when he came home from work. It wasn't unusual for them not to see each other even if they were in the house together a long time. Neil wanted to be by himself, and they let him. He told me about going up into the room calling for him because he hadn't come out to take the phone, which was from a worried friend at school, and about Neil lying on his mattress, a pool of blood round his head drying.

I took over the responsibility for the funeral arrangements and all the hassles on the phone and at the door. I also took the job of cleaning Neil's room. I think me being there quickly was very important to my parents. I hadn't wanted to come at all at first. I wanted just to go off somewhere alone for a long time.

In one of the letters Neil left he said those who don't understand what he'd done should ask me, because I was the closest to him. He also said he wanted to be cremated and his ashes given to me in Chicago where I would scatter them. I was perplexed . . . because I partly felt that I did actually know better than anyone what had been going on in him to bring him to suicide; I also felt that I knew almost nothing about Neil or why he would kill himself.

For the superficial, immediate cause, I told my parents it was probably a romantic fantasy that climaxed too precipitously to be stopped at the last moment—that if he'd been able to experience what he was doing instead of dying instantly, or almost instantly, he would have reversed himself.

I told myself that he manifested the climate of the whole country then, of the season.

There were no reasons but huge futile ones. I managed to rail against the school and the city and his pathetically shallow friends. I myself saw dozens of scenes develop from the past where I had failed Neil. I don't know what thing or things could have saved him.

I went back to school. I couldn't get my equilibrium all that year. The smallest things could bring on deep depressions. Don and I drew apart. My father's illness came as an extension of Neil's death, as a consequence of my father's being caught too close to the horror.

And I read the poems over and thought what I was feeling and noticing in the season and the world, and floating on, Neil was feeling and doing and sinking in.

I'm writing this in Florida after a year, where there is no autumn, and it is warmer now than it was in "Okeover" in August. I have never before avoided this season and I have been thinking a lot about what it means to go into winter where there is no dying of vegetation and the changes in the earth are small.

It is easy now to imagine my brother, unchanged in his coffin, buried in my clothes. Carefully tended, his long hair, much smoother than mine, combed over the hole in his left temple (He was left-handed so naturally enough he held the little .32 in that hand, the gun barely capable of doing its job.), and the unerased look of hurt around his mouth. I share lips that pout like that with him. Will mine express such pain at being unloved as his did, when I die?

In Adam's writing about Neil's death we can feel the impact of the shock. We can also see how a totally unexpected tragedy can plunge someone into expected action. Even in a state of shock the expectation was to be with his parents, to both be supportive and responsible for duties. This was perhaps not his need—more likely his parents'. It seems his need was to be alone. His was for more information: Why, How, What, etc . . . So what he needed was information and solitude, neither of which he was able to get at that time. Instead, because his parents needed information that they hoped he could provide (and could not), he gave what he could to them. He even supplied an explanation of which he was not sure.

It seems siblings often assume the responsibility for taking care of things, postponing their own needs. We often see siblings offer explanations to parents because it is expected that children in the same age group must experience things similarly. Parents ask and the remaining sibling feels required to answer. It is as if there is a temporary role reversal.

Soon the brother or sister may begin to identify with the dead sibling, begin to feel depressed, assume that he may be doomed to die by suicide also. The fight for survival begins.

Adam continues:

> One of us died and one of us went crazy
> and one of us is a no account bum.
> It's my brother who died, Neil, and he killed himself.
> My father went crazy, dying . . . . . .
>
> But then I'm lucky, living, which Neil isn't.
> With enough time to work, providing I keep working,
> on preventing what drove my father nuts, driving me nuts,
> which if I can do and be a no account bum, Okay . . . . .
>
> Neil, whatever it was in us
> that went off in you, it has disarmed me,
> because already one of us has died
> and one of us gone crazy and
>
> I can't guarantee that when I reach 51, I won't have stored
> in me enough shame and guilt at things done and never done or
> contemplated
> and never achieved to swamp and kill me.
> But I've seen it once, and more important, recognized it in myself.

It is common as part of the confusion, depression, and desire to escape from pain, that a survivor will sleep a great deal.

> There are no paths through grief—
> though I and others
> have discovered a sleep cure
> where sleep, a slice of death,
> a journey toward the centre of the earth,
> is beloved
> and into which I sink gladly
> at first for annihilation
> but discovering a passage of some kind
> into an after-life of dreams . . .
>
> Second Anniversary of Neil's suicide

A fragment of a dream—

> Neil gives or sends me a poem, full of self-anguish, and I recognize the
> handwriting as my script from my early teens.

Adam, having a problem seeing himself as both the same and
different from Neil, told of another dream.

> I dreamt of digging into his grave—needing contact, and saw myself
> holding his body. As I held him he crumbled into ashes. That's when I
> realized that I was alive and he was dead.

It is now 1983, and things have changed for Adam, but the
visual and emotional impact of his writing reinforces the concept
that only someone who has experienced such pain can truly
understand and identify with it. His willingness to expose that
part of himself to help others understand will, one would hope,
accomplish just that.

There are other problems to be faced that we must mention
also. When a child in a family kills himself, it seems that parents
sometimes have a strong need to protect the other children in the
family from outsiders—from what they feel might be upsetting
questions from well-meaning but inquisitive neighbours, friends,
and teachers. So it is difficult to find much information on the
kinds of pain that brothers and sisters of a suicide experience.
Family messages get relayed to the children in subtle ways.
Brothers and sisters of whatever age may be shackled with inhibited
grief work because the family may prohibit grief. "Get on with
it" may be the dominant message. Sometimes the remaining children are told by the parents that the one who killed himself was
"sick," meaning crazy. Insanity does not add to his social status
or acceptability with his friends or increase his own feeling of
personal worth. Instead it may create fears—will he also become
"sick" and kill himself? There are several diseases, such as
epilepsy, that attack children of the same family. Both the parents
and the surviving children may fear that suicide is such a disease.
The child who hears half-truths and innuendos about the suicide
of a brother or sister and at the same time witnesses the intensity
of his parents' grief will likely become even more fearful and
forlorn.

Reactions of outsiders to the family can be extremely painful to
the youngster who is questioning and grieving. As an adolescent,
rejection and ostracism are especially traumatic.

Ben talked about going back to high school after his brother Brian shot himself. He vividly remembers an incident when he was in the cafeteria with a group of kids, and they wanted to call out to a friend who had the same name as his brother. Mention of the name Brian, even though directed at another boy, was too embarrassing, so they got up and walked over instead of calling out.

Ben: "They never again mentioned his name, and it was as if he had never existed at all! Our friends stopped doing things with me, too; I no longer existed for them either. I was a reminder of their guilt because they didn't know, hadn't been able to help."

There is another sensation that may flicker and then settle within the recesses of the bereaved who tries to pick up again his own place in society; and that is an underlying sense of notoriety. After all, it certainly makes a person conspicuous when his brother shoots himself. People take notice, and the survivor becomes a prominent figure for awhile, and although it is because of a terrible and painful incident, being noticed changes how one feels about oneself in yet another way. It reinforces "you" and this can, in spite of everything, be enjoyable. It's hard to admit, even to oneself, that there can be anything even remotely enjoyable about the death of a loved one; and so, another feeling to be guilty about. For the teen-ager this can come during a rebellious state. It's a time of looking for ways to shock authority, to be different from society, and still band together with peer groups. Antisocial teens often form a kind of cult or group where the initiation rite is a problem at home. The brother or sister of a suicide qualifies and can use this notoriety to gain acceptance and approval among this particular peer group.

Opposite to, and at the same time closely tied to, the notoriety is the feeling of shame. Ben stated over and over—"people think there's something wrong with our family and it reflects on me." So we now come to the adolescent's need to protect his parents and their status in the community.

It hurts the other children deeply to have their friends or teachers or anyone in the community gossip about the family. The brothers or sisters who live with and love the parents and witness their pain and mourning want to help them feel better. If they are aware of accusations or insinuations from others, they feel anger and shame. They want to shout, "We *are* a normal family! We do not hide a terrible secret; we do not do horrible things; and we are not crazy!"

Parents shielding children, children protecting parents—family relationships change and new alliances form. The absence of one member causes a shift in the family balance that can have positive repercussions. A new kind of closeness, companionship, and love can develop. Sandra said one of the things that helped her kids was that there was a "lot of love blowing around the house."

At the same time as the new closeness forms between certain family members, blame may remain buried and surface at unexpected times. Now the remaining children blame both the parents and themselves. If they were no longer living at home, "What was going on in my family that my brother killed himself?" can be a question that hovers around for years.

"Did my parents overprotect, or reject, or ignore my brother?" What is often a harder query is, "Why did they favour me?"

"Did I manipulate them into giving me more?"

"Why did I let them accuse him when it was my fault?"

Psychiatrists say all young children have death wishes towards their siblings, especially younger ones. These usually occur at times of jealousy and anger. If a child remembers his death wish and sees it come true, how can he not blame himself somewhere deep inside?

Relationships between brothers and sisters are very complex. Kids often complain that the younger one follows them around like a shadow and imitates whatever they do. Having a shadow disappear from one's life leaves a person feeling as if part of him has gone, or has been cut off. A person can spend a great deal of time searching for that shadow in order to feel whole and complete again. An ally against the parents or against the outside world has left you to do battle alone. We have heard brothers and sisters say of the one who died, "He was the most like me," "It was as if we were twin souls," "If one of us had to be suicidal, why him and not me?"

But the sibling is not always a friend and ally. At times he is the one who arouses the most jealousy and need to compete. There is a big difference between being in the "middle" of a family or in the "centre" of a family. In a whole and complete family a child can be in the middle and be part of it but equal to the older brothers or sisters. When one dies by suicide, the one left becomes the centre, the hub around which the family focuses its attention. He may become overprotected because he is now seen as more precious, or he may become special in other ways. All the family's expectations may be directed at the remaining child. He may be attributed with the qualities of the suicide victim and unrealistic demands placed upon him. Alternatively the family may scapegoat the other child —constantly compare him with an idealized version of the child who died. This centre may not be a comfortable place to be, or if it is, it may also be a guilty place because you arrived there through the death of your brother or sister.

Whether the survivor is a young child, teenager, or an adult with one's own family—when losing a brother or sister to suicide— all seem to go through the same bereavement process with the same feelings occurring at different times. Perhaps the loss is more intense if the child who killed himself was an adolescent because he was alive for so short a time.

Adam once said a lot of his pain centered around the fact that Neil would never grow up with him, have sex, have children, and be his lifelong friend. So Adam's loss is also for what might have been. He became a day-care counsellor, camp director, little league coach, and even occasionally slipped and called his dog Neil. But he could not find Neil.

> We have come to sit together on a rooftop
> while everything is falling from the trees.
> I cannot see your face. Your voice
> behind me rattles like the leaves.
> I realize I do not know you
> or what in this season kills you.
>
> I have taken a lot for granted,
> being the older brother,
> but I have always depended on you
> to want to stay alive.

What I never felt the need to do
What I know I will never be able to do
is find your hand
to turn your face to me
to turn and face you
to say "please stay with me."
Your voice has ended with the leaves
and you are the flint of a pistol in my hand.

Then Adam dreamt a lot about joining Neil. After a time Adam was able finally to accept the fact that Neil was dead, and he no longer tried to follow him. Instead he carried Neil around with him, and brother or not, he was heavy.

You are on a hospital cot,
a kind made of aluminum
and riding on wheels
and you are, of course, lifeless.
I wheel you about the rooms
of my life,
parking you unobtrusively
as unobtrusively as ever a corpse is,
in the corners.
I scarcely look at you
yet now and then I reach
an arm out sideways
to adjust your position.
It is actually a fairly comfortable relationship
though I haven't the slightest idea
what I get out of it
unless it's some mimicry of companionship
or simply something to occupy my time.

And finally it became possible to let him go. One way Adam found to do that was to let Neil speak to him in his mind. Neil speaks:

Here time runs differently, I think, more slowly. I am not as much older as you have become, and yet I change too—out of what I came from. Now I can see you, Adam, and know I never meant to hurt you—not this much, not this long—for what I did.

But please realize, if I could wish to be alive again, and I don't, it would be because I wished my own life, not because I missed you, your love, the promise of knowing you further. I had those things before also, and maybe I found them hard to see, but nevertheless they existed, and they weren't enough to keep me alive. Oh, perhaps you could have given me more. But if I had truly possessed the self-love that now is all that could make me wish to live, you could have given me far less and I would have still fought fiercely to live.

Though Neil was still with Adam somewhat, Adam was beginning the recovery. He was no longer floundering in grief feelings that were hindering his recovery.

He was on his way!

These dreams, so alive to me
now spit me back to the bright world
with its mundane amazements
and sunlit miracles.

Adam stopped dreaming about Neil—stopped seeing his alive face or his dead body every night. In fact, Adam stopped sleeping as much as he had been and began to feel alive.

Chapter IX

REACHING AND RECOVERING

There's never been a time I felt such sorrow.
It comes in waves, some large, some small;
But each one having its own impact
On the rock I'm supposed to be.
How long, how far,
Does my grief have to go,
Before I start to move?
                    —Survivor
              Three weeks after death of loved one

Recovery from grief is an ongoing process, and so too is the activity of helping others recover. Counsellors also search. Not for answers as to why the suicides occur, but how—how those mourning a suicide death can best be helped? The author's need to help surfaced as a response to requests from people who were asking for general information about suicide. As the authors probed, it was discovered that many of these requests came from people grieving a suicide death, and they needed as much information as they could get. Later it was discovered that they often devoured books in their search for answers. This became one way they could help as they collected books and shared sometimes huge bibliographies with the authors. What they found together was that most of the books were religious in orientation or theoretical in design and did not offer much solace. The religious orientation was not often helpful, because with the suicide death disillusionment with God sometimes accompanied grief. Sometimes survivors turned to religion for answers and found instead platitudes that were far from comforting. Maryanne said, "I've always gone to church and believed that I would find solace there. But when I asked for reasons I was told not to question. Twice I was told by two different learned people of the church, whom I respected, that as long as I

84

questioned "why" his (my husband's) soul would not be able to rest, and that I had to stop questioning. But I wasn't ready to stop, and so I felt even more guilty."

Although many survivors find emotional strength through religion, many have never turned to religion and find it difficult to do so. Often, survivors turn to the medical profession. The men and women in this profession are dedicated to preventing illness and death, and often spend their professional lives questioning themselves; "If only he had come to me earlier . . . If only I had ordered more tests . . . If only I had sent him for a referral or X-ray, etc . . . Could I have prevented the death?" So they too, if honest with themselves, when one of their patients dies by his own hand might feel they missed clues and feel guilty about that. Or doctors might indeed be angry at someone who has chosen to die, when the doctor has spent his life trying to help people who *want* to live and sometimes can't. So the bereaved must often look elsewhere for the support he needs. That is where counselling came in. It seemed appropriate that the authors try and impart some of what they knew about suicide to those who were searching for answers.

As was mentioned previously, the bereavement process in the event of a suicide has several stages. In the first stage there is often shock and disbelief. This denial often delays the impact of the loss but may be an important survival mechanism. If one cannot deny, one may sink into despair. During this time people behave mechanically—making arrangements, doing what needs to be done, but keeping an emotional distance from others to avoid feeling the pain of the loss. This period varies in time from person to person, usually lasting for at least a few weeks, but possibly continuing for years.

The full impact of the loss may not even be felt until a future loss occurs. In other words, the pain may be covered over until at another time the survivor is faced with losing someone or something important and he over-reacts. It is as if this minor loss is as tragic as the death was. The old pain was lying dormant, unhealed, and resurfaces.

However, most people will usually stay in this state of shock briefly before they begin to question. In this first stage of mourning, it appears strangers are not welcome. The shock and disbelief need time to wear off, and survivors are not ready to allow themselves the pain that comes later. In this initial period, it is often important for friends and helpers to respect a survivor's desire for privacy while at the same time conveying they're ready to talk or help when the survivor is ready. Once the questioning begins, it seems it is important for close friends and family to be around to help take over the physical chores and try to answer the practical questions.

"What should I say to people who phone and ask to speak to him?"

"How do I answer the mail that comes addressed to her?"

"What should I do with his guitar?"

These questions are difficult to answer. Perhaps the most helpful thing to remember when responding is "do not make any major decisions now." Do not sell the house and move, do not give away personal belongings, do not write accusing letters, and above all, do not deny what happened to people who inquire. Do only what is comfortable, what you can handle at this time, and wait. Wait for the time to be right to make decisions based on carefully thought out ideas and emotionally felt needs.

Later on, some people make decisions to move, some to stay; some to give away many belongings and keep only special items; some want to give away everything or give things to special friends of the deceased. Decisions are very individual; whether to hang pictures or put away all remembrances—and different solutions satisfy different people. There are no *shoulds*. At this early time in the mourning process, the friend and helper can ask, "What do you want to do?" and if there is no burning need, "Can you postpone that decision for now?"

There are some decisions that need to be made in this initial period, and it is a time for family members to make those decisions together. To be buried or cremated, what to say in the eulogy and who should be notified, etc., making these decisions together lays the cornerstone for grieving together later. It seems that information given at this time about where to turn for help when ready is comforting, and can be filed away for future reference.

As he moves into the second stage of mourning, the survivor craves information about suicide in general and pleads for answers as to why his specific loved one chose to die. The authors found they could help with general information, and that this did in fact help people to begin to talk. Talking about suicide enables people to talk about their feelings about *the* suicide. In this second stage, the feelings of anger, guilt, and self-blame occur. Now it is crucial that the bereaved have someone to express their intimate feelings to, and at the same time know their feelings are common. Now is the time when two very important emotional states emerge, and it is very comforting to know they are prevalent. The survivor feels he is going crazy or he feels suicidal himself. Because he is confused, preoccupied with the death, often not sleeping or eating, the mourner feels out of place. Because he often "sees" and "talks to" the loved one, the survivor may think he is going crazy. "Sometimes when I'm driving I forget what day or year it is, or where I am, and I panic."

This was covered earlier, and is worth mentioning again. Now he may need hospitalization, and the friends, doctors, and counsellors must be prepared to consider this for a short time. Sometimes the bereaved may imitate the behaviour of the loved one before he died. The survivor may even take on some of the same personality characteristics. This is because the mourner has a need to keep the loved one alive and near him to keep from feeling abandoned. But if the bereaved adopts depressed behavior, he may become suicidal. Almost all the bereaved that were interviewed felt suicidal at one time and did not talk to anyone about their suicidal thoughts when they were occurring.

When the bereaved talk about their sadness or loss, anger and blame, fears and pain, they are learning to cope with these feelings and are moving towards the third stage. In this stage they will begin to let go and reenter life with old memories and new strengths, to begin to live again.

Just as there are three general stages in grieving, three stages of support are also helpful. Just as people move into different stages of mourning at different times, so, too, people are ready to experience one or more of the support stages at different times.

When the survivor is ready to communicate his feelings, he needs people with whom he feels safe and people who will not rush him, allowing him all the time he needs. For some, family

and friends can provide this. For people without access to professional help, a friendly smile or an offer of help can be a life
support.

Friends can help the mourner express his feelings of sadness,
yearning, anger, guilt, etc. by reassuring the mourner that these
are all normal grief feelings and that talking will help. The listener
can also encourage the mourner to talk about the circumstances of
the death and his reactions to it. The bereaved also need to find
someone who will listen to his recitation of the history of the relationship between the suicide victim and the one mourning him. All
the "I remembers" are important to express. There may be feelings
about previous losses that are induced by the present bereavement.
For example: "When my father died it was different..." The
listener can ask, "How?" and the process of unburdening pent up
emotions can begin again.

A friend who offers support through a time of crisis needs to be
aware that the friendly relationship has altered for a time. The survivor may be the needy one for a long time, in what, by definition
of friendship, is a reciprocal relationship. It is also difficult, because in this temporarily restructured relationship the friend cannot express his own ideas about the death or opinions about the
dead person. Many survivors get even more confused with too
much input from well-meaning friends. The listener's feelings
about the suicide victim are not important at this time.

Men, women, and children have different "ways of being" with
friends, as well as culturally different ways of responding to loss.
Friends and family members offering support need to remember
this. Men prefer to remain anonymous and are more likely, if they
reach out at all, to reach for a comparative stranger. They have a
lot of difficulty expressing vulnerability and sadness. Anger is
much more acceptable for men to express. Women are more comfortable with tears and with asking for help. It often appears as if
women mourn longer, but probably it is that they are not as quiet
about it. Children do not have as much experience with loss and so
have even less developed coping mechanisms. Children want to
know what changes will occur in their physical structure as a
result of the death. Will they have to move or change schools or
bedrooms? Will Mom now have to work? Children may continue

for a long time to fantasize that the person who died is still alive and will come back. Friends need to remember this is normal and not accuse the child of lying.

Often, about six weeks to three months after the death, family and friends tire, feel exasperated, and begin to withdraw their emotional support. The authors tried a specific approach. Step one in their professional helping process is to provide individual counselling at this time. In individual sessions, the mourner can express what he considers both negative and positive feelings without being judged. He can be encouraged to remember the loved one as he really was—through talking about his blemishes and imperfections as well as his virtue and merit. He can be urged to continue viewing him in balance when talking with his family. This will prevent forming a shrine and will prevent grieving becoming a life-style. Writing (letters, poetry, journals) appears to be healing for many and is suggested at this stage. Now, too, it is important for the counsellor to look at other losses the survivor has had in his life and how he has coped with those. It has been found that rather than regular weekly sessions, the survivors prefer, after approximately four to six sessions, to come sporadically when they feel the need (depending on what is happening in their lives). This frequency gradually diminishes. The authors also make themselves available twenty-four hours a day for phone calls, so that the mourner never has to feel panic-stricken or overwhelmed by feelings of isolation. Interestingly, the survivors were determined to "cope as well as they could" between sessions and seldom called in crisis.

The bereaved's role and self-concept both have changed because of the death. "I thought I was a good wife. Now I'm no longer a wife and I couldn't have been a good one, or he wouldn't have left me. So I'm angry at him for negating everything I believed and everything I had."

This impotent rage must be explored in the individual sessions with the survivor so he can stop feeling both responsible and guilty. Through the relationship with the counsellor the mourner can get back some self-esteem while learning how to once again form a trusting relationship. There comes a time, however, when this connection needs to be expanded. The need to meet other survivors often becomes intense.

Workshops were instituted, consisting of ten to twelve people who had lost different members of their family at different times. This was found to be extremely beneficial for the bereaved. A mother who had never talked to her daughter about her father's death could be comforted and encouraged by a daughter in the workshop who wished *her* mother would talk to *her*. The patterns of connections that form are intricate, and people touch each other in unusual ways over simple things, like common names. The relief is evident, the changes powerful. Often someone will say, "When will I feel better?" and the response can be, "At two years you don't think of them as often, at three years you don't cry on Mother's Day." Just knowing it does change is amazing medicine!

The workshops have a purpose. They are designed to move people from repeating the same questions to themselves and giving themselves the same answers. As if a record has been stuck in the same groove going around and around, the needle must be lifted and pushed forward. In a new groove they hear something different and respond with a different emotion.

By using structured exercises in a group, the authors explore the survivor's feelings and give them practice sharing these feelings with each other. Images of *self* that they show the world are discussed so they can become aware of how they may contribute to the isolation they feel. It may be suggested that everyone indulge in their fantasy of rejoining their loved one. A lot of time is spent exploring the person who died—how he viewed his own life and death, and his relationship to the person in the workshop. There is a lot of group sharing. The combination of intensity and self-awareness produces a forgotten feeling of aliveness and often a decision to change present relationships. Because reentry into daily routine is difficult after such an experience, time is spent with each person before they leave, checking on the resources they have and giving them a promise that counselling will be available. Also, a follow-up workshop is offered four weeks later. That is approximately the time when they again begin to despair. Also, they are very anxious to see how the others have been and are reluctant to let go of the newfound closeness. At the follow-up workshop everyone gets a chance to talk about what changes occurred afterwards, what feelings they experienced, and what new relationships formed as a result. This is the most exciting time for everyone.

"I was able to talk to my son about what really happened—and he doesn't blame me! We cried together for the first time since it happened eight years ago."

"I was finally able to pick out a headstone and come up with an inscription."

"I was able to pack up and sort out his things that I had buried in the basement."

"My sister wants to come and meet other survivors—she saw how much better I've been feeling."

The mourning has begun to end when the task of cleaning up—emotionally and physically—has been started.

"Help" in bereavement counselling has been defined as responses to statements:

1. "I can't be the only one this happened to."
2. "I can't deal with this alone."
3. "I'm so lonely."
4. "I want to make something change, help others, help make the meaningless death more meaningful."

The workshop responds to the first three statements. The group setting substitutes for the beginnings of reconnection to the larger community. As they reconnect with life, they can break the connection with the dead.

As a further step towards reestablishing ties to their individual community resources, and as a response to statement number four, a bereavement support group was started—a mutual-help network of people who continue to talk about issues that concern them, and at the same time are committed to reaching out to others in the community who need a place to mourn. Membership is open ended and flexible; come when you want, and bring whoever you want.

There are support groups arising throughout the country to deal with a multitude of problems, especially when the particular problem is one that is best understood by others who have experienced it, such as "Widow to Widow."

Mutual-help groups do three main things:

a. They enable the individual to accept himself as someone in a new situation as he identifies with other members.
b. The group provides a role model and information to meet the individual's need to cope with the new situation.
c. It provides opportunity for the individual to change roles from the person receiving and benefiting from help to the one providing it. This reinforces his sense of competence and gives meaning to the previous experience. (Silverman, 1980).

To receive help from a professional reinforces a sense of weakness, since the mourner stays in the role of recipient. But the helper in a mutual-help group is potentially a friend, and the relationship can become reciprocal.

A mutual-help group for people bereaving a suicide death does all this very effectively. There have been groups that have a professional present and groups where the leader and structure come from the members themselves, and both types have been helpful. Although the members are experts about their own feelings and experiences and can certainly offer each other empathy and share their experiences, they may not be as knowledgeable about the bereavement process. The role of the professional in such groups is to help integrate the personal experiences of the members with an overall knowledge of bereavement. (Solomon, 1981) Our mutual-help group wanted a counsellor present, partly because they were concerned about the group process—the dynamics of sensitive people, hurt feelings, tears, or inappropriate responses. As they became more comfortable they took more initiative in conversations, but still wanted someone they could turn to if some imagined difficulty should arise with a new member. Because of their willingness to have one of the authors present, exciting changes have been witnessed.

Statements continually crop up that reinforce the reason for the group's existence:

"All the cards are on the table, and they're now face up."

"After going around and around all these emotions, I end up with compassion for him."

"I feel as if I've been running a marathon, and I'm on the last mile."

"I've exchanged a lead jacket for a light windbreaker."

"I feel like I'm climbing a ladder, and this group is holding the ladder."

"I was afraid to talk to my daughter about her Dad's death because I thought she wouldn't be able to handle it, she'd cry, and I'd cry."

"She might blame me, and since I blamed myself, I wouldn't be able to deny it. So instead I denied her the chance to talk about it, to get more information, and to get closer to me. I guess I was denying her and me, and me and her, because I was afraid!"

Along with verbal statements, behaviour changes were witnessed that signify the end of mourning. Laura was able to give away her husband's drum set and to keep a piece for one of her children. It had taken her four years to decide what to do with it. Another woman was able to visit the cemetery for the first time, years later, and ask some questions aloud that she had never voiced. She heard the responses within her and believed them to be true.

As the group became closer, the survivors were able to look at what may be the most difficult thing of all to accept: the positive changes that came as a result of the death. The resignation had changed to acceptance, and now they were able to consider the gift they had inherited. For some it was personal.

"I'm able to see that I don't have to be perfect—my parents loved my brother, and he wasn't perfect."

"I've become much closer to my mom, and I understand a lot more about communicating feelings."

"I've made some very close friends who really understand me."

For all, the greater appreciation of life, the precious moments, the sharing of joy with loved ones, the value of life itself, became enhanced. For those left alive, the acceptance becomes hope. Perhaps the will to survive is the choice to make the best of a life that has been maimed but not paralyzed.

In an earlier chapter, Adam talked about his brother Neil. He said, "It's like the act is incomplete and you're left with an unanswerable retort, and until you end the conversation, and you can't, you mourn." Now Adam says, "There's still no way I can reply to Neil, but it doesn't seem so much like he's expecting an answer, now."

A Last Look

When I was four years old
I used to wonder what
your voice would sound like once
you started talking.

Seventeen years we were
brothers in one room
my voice, and your voice.
Then you killed yourself
Dad went crazy, died
My grief was stopped
with rage that you could do
such a thing to me.

And there was also fear.
No male in my family
lived but me; I was
twenty-one. Perhaps
my sex could be a poison.
I dug at myself to find
and defang that cobra
if it was there in me.

Unconsciously I tried
living like the dead
regardless of the fact
that it brought us no closer.

But to stay alive
it also seemed I needed
to become a man.
I wanted two men.

Some help in knowing what
a man is like, someone
to help me see myself,
as you had been my ally
when I fought against
Mom, when we were kids.

Wouldn't it have been
fine, if we could have
continued as we had
begun—you letting me
lead the way for us?
But you abandoned me.

I don't know how I came
to bend my back as if
I'd slung your adolescent
body on my shoulders
headed for some Boy's Town
of my mind, carrying
you through my life
unable or unwilling
to look at you or let
you drop, whining that
you wouldn't share the load,

but after years of this
you suddenly appeared
in fantasy, alive
at twenty-four: what kind
of man you would have been.
Bright possibles—I thought
of asking you to live
near me in Vancouver

and the riprap of my anger
gave, and here was grief
and grief and need and all
I hadn't said to you
about my need, about
your tenderness, your voice

and finally here was Adam
who has a voice, who feels
tender and alive.

Today, in fantasy
I raise your body up
just to touch and hold
and say goodbye to.
Maybe I also want
to warm you still, be hugged
by you, but you quickly
decay and I must drop
you back into the earth.

Poor little guy who killed
himself, who is becoming
earth at last, I miss
you and remember you,
I mourn you too, but I
am near the end of mourning.

end

BIBLIOGRAPHY

Silverman, P. R.: Mutual-help groups. *The Psychotherapy Handbook*. Edited by Rickie Herink. Utica, New York, Meridian, 1980.

Solomon, M.: Bereavement from suicide, (Research) in *Canadian Journal of Psychiatric Nursing*. July/Sept. 1981, Vol. 22, pp. 18–19.

EPILOGUE

As we finished this book, wondering if the people whose lives we wrote about had somehow changed by being involved, we asked a few to read the manuscript. It was a difficult thing to do. We were concerned that they might feel too exposed or somehow misrepresented. Also, we were anxious that they might reexperience the pain when reading the book. But we wanted to know if sharing their experiences in this way had somehow helped them. We did not want a testimonial to us, our work, or the book, but rather some confirmation that the picture we described was a true one and that all the problems they had wrestled with had been mentioned.

Everyone we asked was excited about reading the manuscript. We found their comments helpful. We also made some interesting observations of the kinds of feedback we got and from whom. It appears that each survivor had an issue that was more of a specific problem to them as individuals, and they focused on those issues when commenting. It is as if some aspect of the grief process that was particularly troublesome has remained dominant. For some, the discussion began again within the family around their specific concern. They exchanged still more information about their sources of pain. Even though the bereaved felt their emotions triggered, they did not feel reminded that their grieving was incomplete when reading the manuscript; rather, they were aware of how far they had come in their own process.

Laura, who still had not been able to tell her children about their father's suicide, became truly aware for the first time that her children might hear it from others. She renewed her determination to tell them. Laura also had not been in contact with her in-laws since her husband's funeral. Between her reading of the manuscript and our writing of the epilogue, she had met with her mother-in-law and was planning to reintroduce her children to their grandparents. I asked Laura if she had been able to read the book through the eyes of her children or her in-laws. She said she had identified only with the wives in the book on first reading, but would read it again with a different perspective. For Laura there were some things missing in the manuscript. She would like to know about other countries' modern concepts and attitudes towards a suicide. She is interested in religious sects and how they handle a suicide funeral, what survivors have to say about that, and what is said in a Eulogy for such a death. These are questions we cannot answer for her now, but she will do some reading on her own.

Ben has chosen to go into training for a new career in human services. He feels his brother's death has contributed to his new awareness of his sensitivity to others and his desire to help them. Ben said he was comforted to see what he feels written in words, and he felt understood. He hopes that survivors in small towns and isolated places would benefit knowing that what they feel is okay, and that they do not have to feel ashamed.

Hariet said, "A lot of emotions expressed and not expressed (or felt) flowed as I read. I was so aware of my own search for knowledge of suicide, understanding, reasons, etc... and here it was all in one. It recalls feelings that were perhaps subconscious. The poetry touches the finer, deep chords of emotion. It is possible to understand the anguish of the time, the confusion, the void."

She had never felt the anger at her son, only at the helping professionals who failed him. But she had done some soul searching and had not avoided the possibility that she was angry with him. Because of that, she had difficulty with some of the observations on anger as the norm. She again broached the subject with her family. She found that one of her daughters had been angry with her brother. She had put a lot of herself into his growing up, and it seemed wasted. But also, she was relieved afterwards that he was at peace. The feelings of anger and relief were probably a new discussion between mother and daughter.

"Insofar as tears and anger — well, in my case I think my steady flow is pain and sorrow, relief because I can talk about it and some self-pity."

Hariet, who is a religious person, also said, "The main absence in the book is more on religion as a source of strength, yet I am at a loss to suggest just how to touch on it more than you have."

Sandra has continued to strive for more self-awareness. She has taken many growth courses and has become more aware of her own needs and developed her communication skills. She has encouraged other survivors to continue to learn more about themselves. In a warm and friendly manner she has been reaching out and helping many other survivors. She felt the book was important and felt good about her story perhaps being helpful to others.

Adam has evolved into the support group leader. He has continued to volunteer his time, energy, inherent skills, and acquired knowledge to benefit new people coming through our program. He is happy to provide a role model for others. When someone says, "Will I ever stop being angry?" he can say how it happened for him, and others are reassured that it is possible.

Because we hoped that the book might also be useful to professionals, we also asked for feedback from counsellors. Betsy was extremely helpful. Because English is her second language, her interpretation of the words was particularly valuable. Her main concern was around the stigma of mental illness, and we had several long discussions.

Counsellor: You talk about the stigma of suicide and mention fear of insanity. You say sometimes people accuse the suicide victim of being mentally ill as a way of excusing the act of suicide. What about the person who kills himself who *was* mentally ill? It is true one does not have to be crazy to kill oneself, but many psychiatric patients have!

Author: I'm not sure what you are getting at. The medical label doesn't stop the pain and questions for the survivor. But the taboo of mental illness may be something separate to deal with?

Counsellor: Exactly. I'm concerned about the family I'm working with now. I think they'd think they are not the kind of survivors you are talking about. They lost someone who was definitely mentally ill.

Author: How does that make them different? Even those who are mentally ill may have made a deliberate decision about suicide during a moment of clarity!

Counsellor: That's true, but it's the taboo of insanity that the survivors have to live with. If the taboo of mental illness is confronted emotionally at the time of the psychiatric diagnosis, then when the suicide occurs, it is more justification for the act. Then they only have to deal with the taboo of suicide, which in the case of mental illness is not as strong. But if the mourner never looked at his feelings about the diagnosis, then at the time of death he has to confront the extra taboo.

Author: Even in mental illness, death occurs during a crisis and creates a crisis. I don't believe there is much difference to the mourner. He still has to go through his own feelings of grief. The difference perhaps is that the reality of the mental illness of the suicide victim may make the survivor more concerned about his own mental health and the inheritance of insanity. But maybe what that concern will do is make the mourner more ready to seek professional help earlier, to be more aware of early signs of depression in himself, since the stigma about seeking professional help has also shifted in a family with mental illness.

Counsellor: Yes, I think that's so. I also feel I've learned a great deal about survivors. Some issues were not clear to me until I read the book. You defined a layer of looking at it and mapped it well. I looked at some of my own grief experiences, and I feel this book could be helpful to both survivors and counsellors who are willing to confront the painful process of mourning old and recent losses. In recommending it to anyone I'd say: It'll make you cry many times. Take your time to read it. Find the right space and have somebody to talk it over with you.